GREAT BALLOON FUN

FOR THE WHOLE FAMILY

Copyright © 1989 Publications International, Ltd. All rights reserved. This publication may not be reproduced or quoted in whole or in part by mimeograph or any other printed or electronic means, or for presentation on radio, television, videotape, or film without written permission from:

Louis Weber, C.E.O.
Publications International, Ltd.
7373 North Cicero Avenue
Lincolnwood, Illinois 60646

Permission is never granted for commercial purposes.

Manufactured in U.S.A.

h g f e d c b a

ISBN 0-88176-648-8

CONTENTS

Great Balloon Fun for the Whole Family	3
Basic Balloon Skills	4
Round Balloon Fun	10
Jack-o'-Lantern	12
Lemon	13
Heart	14
Grapes	15
Tulips	16
Basic Dog	18
Octopus	20
Dachshund	22
Giraffe	24
Basic Hat	25
Basic Rabbit	28
Pirate's Belt and Sword	30
Elephant	32
Skull	34
Bee	35
Party Hat	38
Swan	40
Bird-Brain Hat	42
Bananas	44
Penguin	46
Beagle	48
Flower Bracelet	50
Cobra	53
Ladybug	55
Scorpion	57
Rabbit in Heart	60
Poodle	63
Pig	66
Tiger	69
Christmas Wreath	72
Teddy Bear	76
Hugs 'n' Kisses	79
Flower	82
Clown	85
Airplane	88
Frog	91
Alien	94
Knight	97
Santa Claus	101
Unicorn	104
Reindeer	107
Baseball Player	110
Paratrooper	113
Fat Clown	114
Butterfly	118
Big Swan	122
Fruit Basket	126

Dave Evans is one of the busiest magicians in Chicago and one of the world's best balloon sculptors. At his magic shows, Dave makes his balloon creations disappear by giving them away. He lives in Chicago Heights, Illinois. Dave designed the balloon sculptures found on pages 12–19, 22–31, and 34–128.

Douglas Wilson is a professional clown who lives in Rolling Meadows, Illinois. Doug designed the balloon sculptures found on pages 20–21 and 32–33.

Photography: Sam Griffith Studios

Balloon sculpting can result in serious injury and can be a dangerous activity. Balloon sculpting should not be attempted in a crowded area. Children under three years old should never be allowed to put an inflated, uninflated, or popped balloon in their mouths. The publisher, authors, and consultants specifically disclaim liability for any loss or injury incurred as a consequence of the use and application, either directly or indirectly, of any advice or information presented herein.

GREAT BALLOON FUN
FOR THE WHOLE FAMILY

Balloons are fun for everyone, and *Great Balloon Fun for the Whole Family* shares the fun with people of all ages. Twisting long thin pencil balloons into the shapes of animals, fruits, flowers, and even Santa Claus is not nearly as difficult as it looks. Once you've mastered a few basic pinches and twists, you'll entertain yourself and your audience by turning balloons into almost anything you can imagine. Even children who are too young to sculpt balloons can join in the fun by adding funny feet and silly stick-on faces to round balloons.

The balloon projects in this book begin with the easiest and progress to more challenging ones. The best way to master balloon sculpting is to work your way through the book from the beginning. But you can also practice the basic balloon skills and start right in with whichever project you want to make. Either way is sure to be lots of fun.

When you've used all the balloons included in this kit, you can purchase more at a balloon or magic store. You'll also need to go to one of these specialty stores for bee balloons and 340 airship balloons, which are used to make a few of the projects in this book.

Get ready for balloon fun. Everything you need is in this kit. Whether you choose to make a huge basket filled with bright balloon fruit, a cute dog, or a round balloon with a bunny face, have fun. Having fun is what balloons are all about.

SAFETY TIPS

Balloons burst!

As everyone knows, balloons can and will pop. You never know when they'll break, but whenever you work or play with balloons be prepared for them to burst. The sting of a popped pencil balloon can hurt more than the snap of a rubber band. Protect your eyes by being ready to turn your head away quickly when your balloon breaks. If you blow up balloons with your breath, keep your hands open to protect your face. When you're making balloon sculptures, ask everyone to give you plenty of room to work. If you're entertaining children, be careful not to point the balloon that you're inflating downward into their faces. Turn slightly away from the children while you blow up balloons. Planning ahead for the inevitable pop is the best way to prevent accidents.

Supervise children!

Children need careful supervision when they're playing with balloons or learning to make balloon sculptures. Never allow a small child to put a balloon in his or her mouth. Inhaling a balloon or a piece of a balloon can be deadly. Children under three years old often put everything they pick up in their mouths, so they are too young to play with balloons of any kind. If there are children around, you need to be especially careful to pick up broken balloon pieces immediately.

It's fun to make hats, masks, and other costumes out of balloons, and you'll find several child-pleasing getups in this book. But children should be warned not to wear balloon hats and masks on their faces and to keep all balloons away from their eyes.

BASIC BALLOON SKILLS

How to Inflate a Balloon

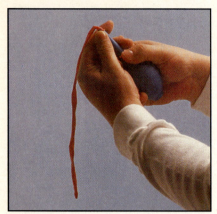  

1. Stretch the balloon a few times before you attempt to inflate it. Slide the nozzle of the balloon over the tip of the pump.

2. Hold the balloon securely in place with your thumb and forefinger. Squeeze and release the pump with your other hand.

3. Pinch the neck of the balloon just above the tip of the pump, and slide it off.

How to Knot a Balloon

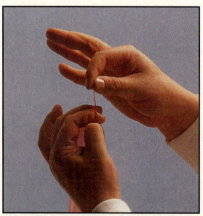 

1. Wrap the nozzle end of the balloon around your forefinger and middle finger. Tuck the nozzle under the balloon between your fingers. Hold the nozzle and pull your fingers out.

2. Don't pull the knot tight.

How to Make a Bubble

Pinch and twist the balloon at least three times. Twist the long part of the balloon, not the bubble, and always twist in the same direction.

How to Make a Twist-Connect

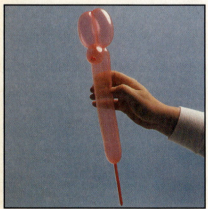

A twist-connect joins two or more bubbles.

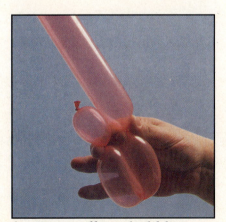

1. Twist off two bubbles and fold them together.

2. Twist the bubbles together at least three times.

5

How to Make a Pinch-Twist

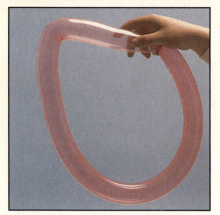

A pinch-twist puts a right angle in an inflated balloon.

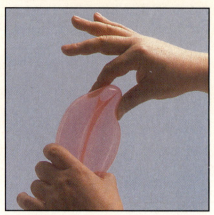

1. Fold the balloon.

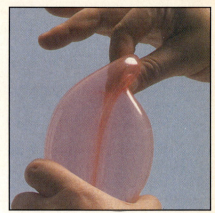

2. Pinch the fold, and twist it gently two or three times.

How to Make a Hook-Twist

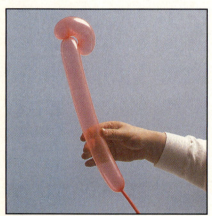

A hook-twist is a long curved bubble.

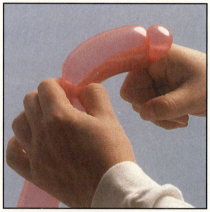

1. Use your forefinger to push the knot into the balloon as far as you can.

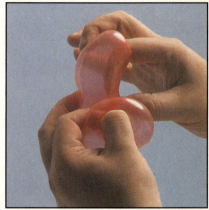

2. Grab the knot with the fingers of your other hand, and carefully roll the balloon off your forefinger.

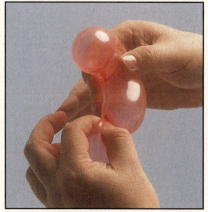

3. Twist this funny-looking bubble at least three times.

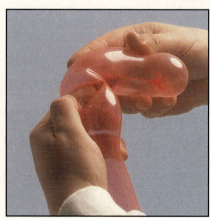

4. Push the knot into the bubble a quarter of the way.

How to Make a Fold-Twist

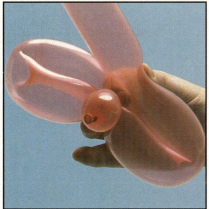

Fold-twists are often used to make arms and legs.

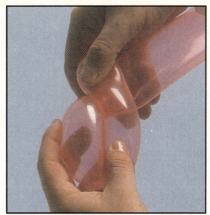

Fold a long bubble on itself, and twist-connect.

How to Make a Poodle-Tail Twist

A poodle-tail twist is a decorative bubble at the tip end of a balloon.

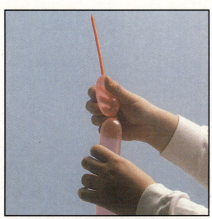

1. Twist off a bubble.

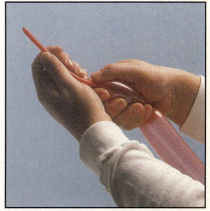

2. Cradle the tail of the balloon with the fingers of one hand.

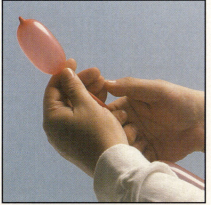

3. With your other hand, squeeze the bubble hard to force air from the bubble into the tip of the tail.

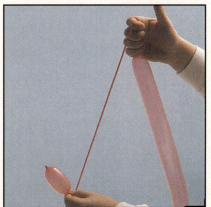

4. Hold the air in the bubble at the tail's end. Stretch the balloon and release it quickly. This helps keep the bubble in the balloon's tail.

How to Make an Ear-Twist

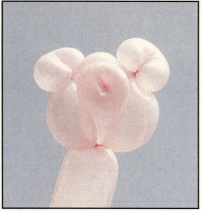
An ear-twisted bubble looks like a teddy bear's ear.

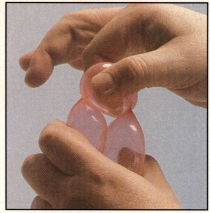
Pinch a small bubble in half, and twist it clockwise at least three times.

How to Make a Pop-Twist

A pop-twist locks off and separates two parts of a balloon. It's used to make arms, legs, and antlers.

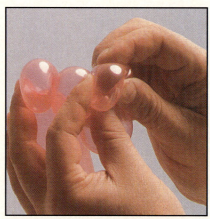
1. A pop-twist requires three bubbles. Ear-twist the first and third bubbles.

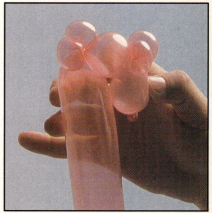
2. Twist the ear-twisted bubbles in half. Be careful because the bubbles are very tight at this point.

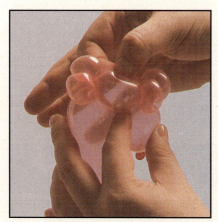
3. Pop the bubble between the two double ear-twisted bubbles.

How to Make an Apple-Twist

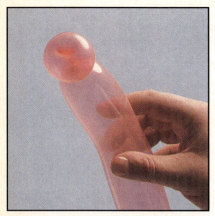

An apple-twist is a bubble with the balloon's knot pushed inside it.

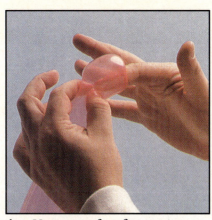

1. Use your forefinger to push the knot into an inflated balloon.

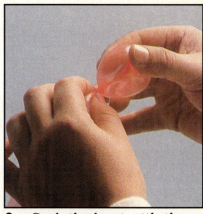

2. Grab the knot with the fingers of your other hand. Remove your forefinger, and twist the bubble at least three times.

BALLOON IDEAS

A flower bracelet can also be a napkin ring.

Pirates' swords and belts set a buccaneer theme for a child's birthday party.

Hang a balloon Christmas wreath on your door.

Make a balloon party hat for everyone who comes to your party. You won't find a better ice breaker.

Decorate a package with balloon tulips instead of a bow.

Present your mom with a bunch of tulips on Mother's Day.

Make a fruit basket filled with balloon fruit to decorate your table for Sunday brunch or Thanksgiving dinner.

Put your sweetheart's favorite balloon animal in a heart for Valentine's Day.

Balloon animals make terrific prizes for party games.

Decorate a tree for your Christmas party with lights and balloon animals. Don't forget to hang several balloon Santas on your tree.

Take along a balloon flower and turn a hospital visit into a party.

Use scary skulls and balloon jack-o'-lanterns to decorate for Halloween.

A balloon teddy bear looks like he's holding a bunch of balloons when you pull the stems of several tulips through his arm.

You'll be a hit at your school carnival, if you make balloon animals for the children.

Instead of buying party favors, teach your guests how to make a balloon animal to take home from your party.

Write your guests' names on balloons instead of place cards.

Float balloon swans in a swimming pool or wading pool.

Decorate a newlywed's car with balloon teddy bears and flowers.

Fill a basket with balloon rabbits and flowers for an Easter centerpiece.

ROUND BALLOON FUN FOR EVERYONE

Round balloons are fun just to bat around, but they also make wonderful party decorations. Small children can decorate round balloons with the funny stickers included in this kit. More skilled balloon sculptors may want to turn a round balloon into a jack-o'-lantern, or they may wish to include round balloons in their sculptures as we did in the paratrooper and the fat clown. Round balloons can also be made into bases for centerpieces. You'll find out how to do this in the instructions for Hugs 'n' Kisses.

Inflating Round Balloons

Stretch the balloon a few times, and inflate it with your breath. Be sure to shield your face with your open hands. Knot the balloon by wrapping its nozzle end around your forefinger and middle finger. Tuck the nozzle under the balloon between your fingers. Hold on to the nozzle and pull your fingers out.

Supervise children when they are first learning to inflate balloons, and encourage younger children to ask you to inflate their balloons.

Making a Balloon Stand on Its Own Feet

Pull the knot of a tied-off balloon through the hole in a pair of feet.

Using Stickers

Peel the self-sticking noses, eyes, and ears off their backing, and press them gently onto a round balloon to make a funny face.

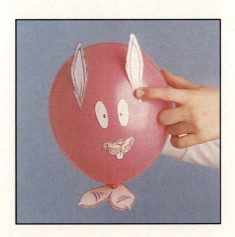

11

JACK-O'-LANTERN

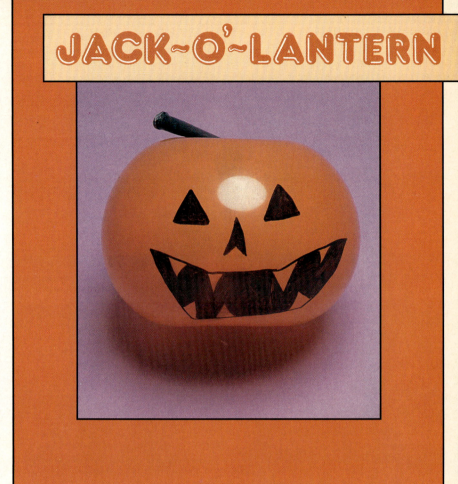

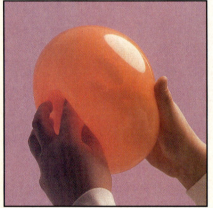

1. Begin by inflating a round balloon. Before you tie it off, let out some air to leave a stem near the nozzle. Knot the balloon.

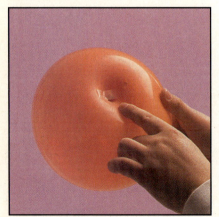

2. Turn the balloon so that the knot is at the bottom. Push the knot into the balloon with your forefinger until you can grab the knot with the fingers of your other hand, and twist.

3. Use transparent tape to attach the knot to the bottom of the balloon.

4. A scrap from another balloon forms the pumpkin's stem.

5. Use a laundry marker to draw a scary face on your jack-o'-lantern.

LEMON

1. To make a lemon, you need a 3½-inch oblong balloon, which you can purchase at a toy or balloon store.

2. Inflate the balloon, and tie it off.

3. Cut off and discard the nozzle end.

HEART

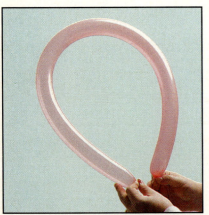

1. Begin by fully inflating a balloon. Form a loop and tie both ends together.

2. Using both hands, pull the top of the loop toward the tied ends to form a heart.

3. Hold the folded balloon and slightly twist the point of the fold.

GRAPES

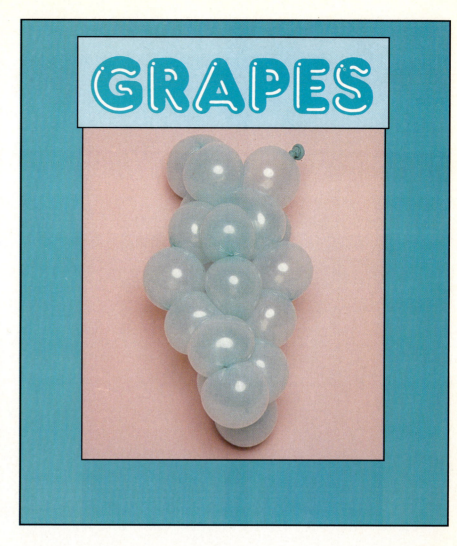

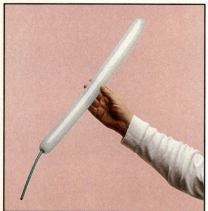

1. Begin by inflating a balloon, leaving a 7-inch tail.

2. Twist off 1-inch bubbles.

3. Continue twisting 1-inch bubbles until you run out of balloon.

4. Twist-connect the first and last bubbles.

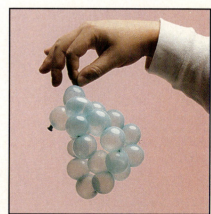

5. Twist-connect other bubbles to form a bunch of grapes.

TULIPS

1. Start by inflating a balloon only 2½ inches.

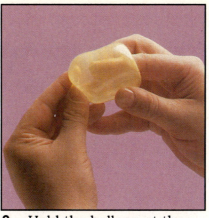

2. Hold the balloon at the end of its tail. Use the forefinger of your other hand to push the knot into the balloon, as shown. Grasp the knot and hold it firmly.

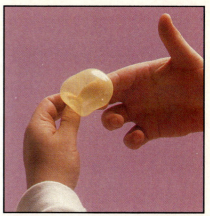

3. Gently remove your forefinger from the balloon.

4. Hold on to the knot, and twist it at least three times.

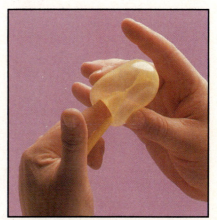

5. Push the knot into the bubble to hold the tulip in place.

6. Make tulips with many colors of balloons, so you'll have a bright bunch.

17

BASIC DOG

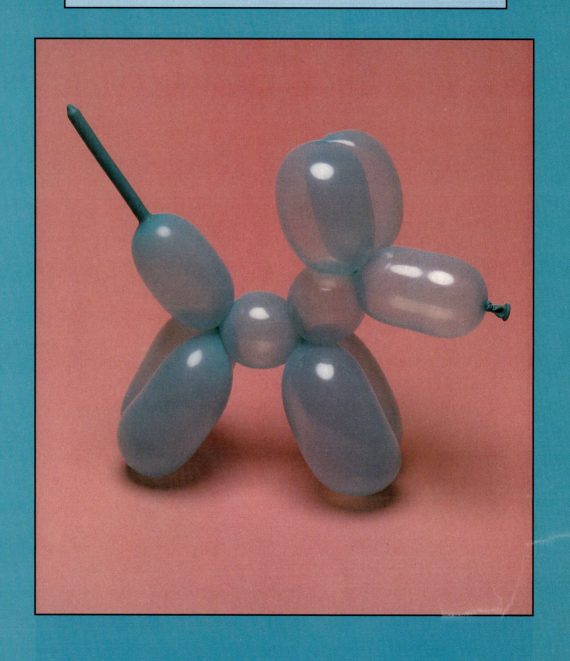

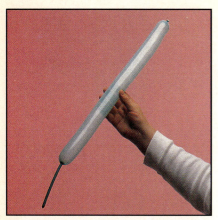
1. Begin by inflating a balloon, leaving a 5-inch tail.

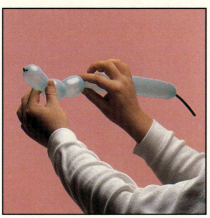
2. Twist off three 2-inch bubbles.

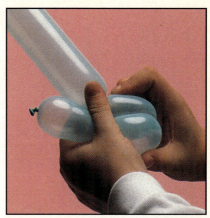
3. Twist-connect the last two 2-inch bubbles.

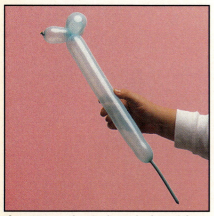
4. Your dog's head should look like this.

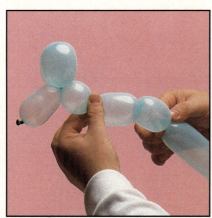
5. Twist off three more 2-inch bubbles.

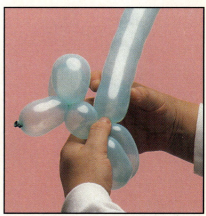
6. Twist-connect the last two 2-inch bubbles, as shown.

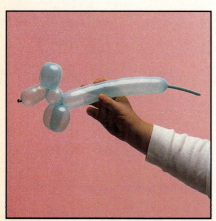
7. The front half of your dog should look like this.

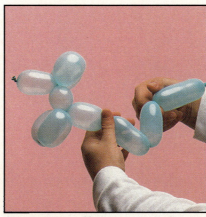
8. Twist off three 2-inch bubbles.

9. Twist-connect the last two 2-inch bubbles to complete your dog.

1. Begin by inflating four balloons, leaving a 1-inch tail on each balloon.

2. Fold-twist one balloon in the middle to form a 3-inch loop.

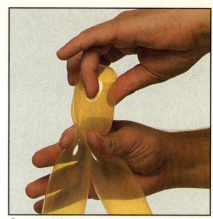
3. Fold-twist another balloon in the middle to form a 1-inch loop.

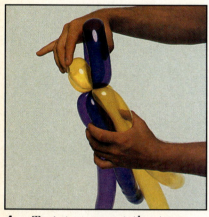
4. Twist-connect the two loops. Arrange the loops so that the 3-inch loop is on top and the 1-inch loop is on the bottom.

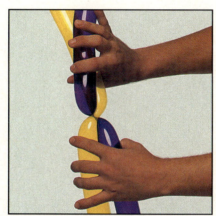
5. Twist-connect the two other balloons, as shown.

6. Twist-connect all four balloons, keeping the 3-inch loop on top.

7. Arrange the tentacles to complete your octopus.

DACHSHUND

1. Begin by inflating a balloon, leaving a 3-inch tail.

2. Twist off three 2-inch bubbles.

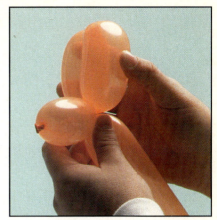
3. Twist-connect the three bubbles to form the dachshund's head and ears.

4. Twist off one 1-inch bubble and two 3-inch bubbles.

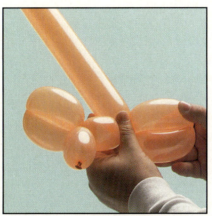
5. Twist-connect the three bubbles to form the dachshund's neck and front legs.

6. Twist off one long bubble and two 3-inch bubbles.

7. Twist-connect the two 3-inch bubbles to finish your dachshund.

8. A quick twist, and a dachshund becomes a giraffe.

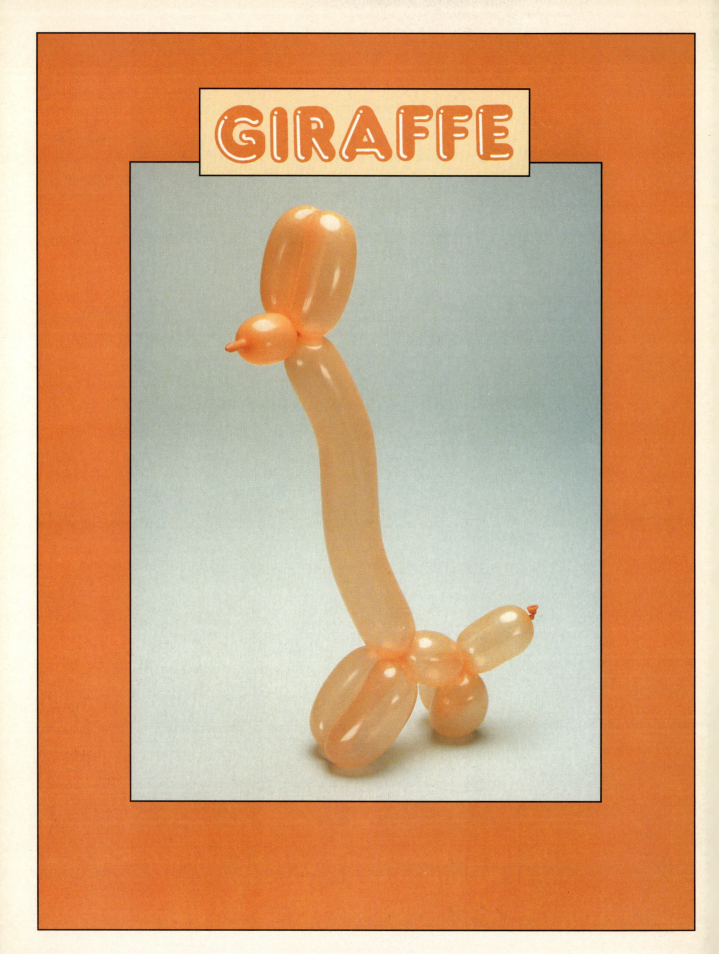

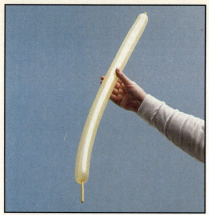

1. Begin by inflating a balloon, leaving a 3-inch tail.

2. Twist off a small bubble near the nozzle, then fold the balloon as shown.

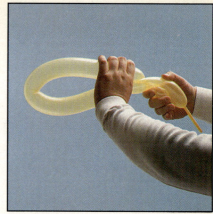

3. Twist-connect the fold with the small bubble, leaving a 3-inch tail at the end of the balloon.

4. Twist off a 2-inch bubble. Hold the bubble with one hand, and cradle the tail with your other hand.

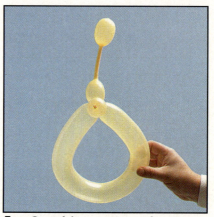

5. Quickly squeeze the 2-inch bubble to force air into the tip of the balloon's tail.

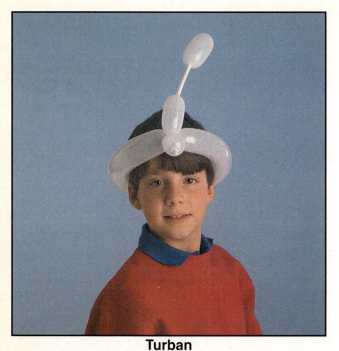

Turban

Wear the hat with the tail in front.

Indian Headdress

Wear the hat with the tail in back, pointing up.

Davy Crockett Hat

Wear the hat with the tail in back, pointing down.

Headset

Wear the hat with the tail down and next to your ear; pull the tail bubble toward your mouth.

BASIC RABBIT

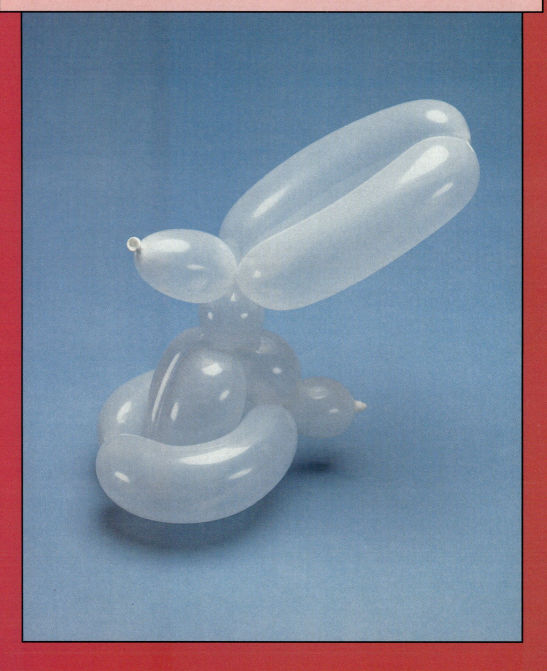

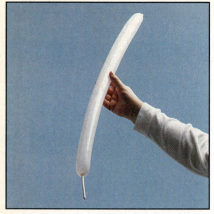
1. Begin by inflating a balloon, leaving a 3-inch tail.

2. Twist off one 2-inch bubble and two long bubbles.

3. Twist-connect the two long bubbles.

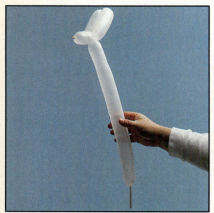
4. Your rabbit's head and ears should look like this.

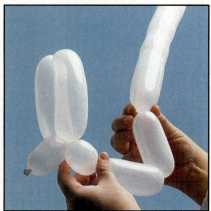
5. Twist off one 1-inch bubble and two 3-inch bubbles.

6. Twist-connect the two 3-inch bubbles.

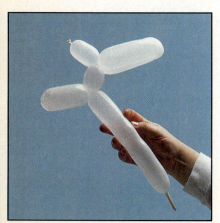
7. Your rabbit's neck and front legs should look like this.

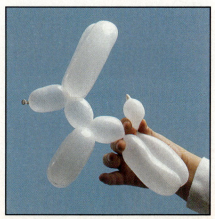
8. Twist off one 2-inch bubble and two 3-inch bubbles.

9. Twist-connect the two 3-inch bubbles to complete your rabbit.

PIRATE'S BELT AND SWORD

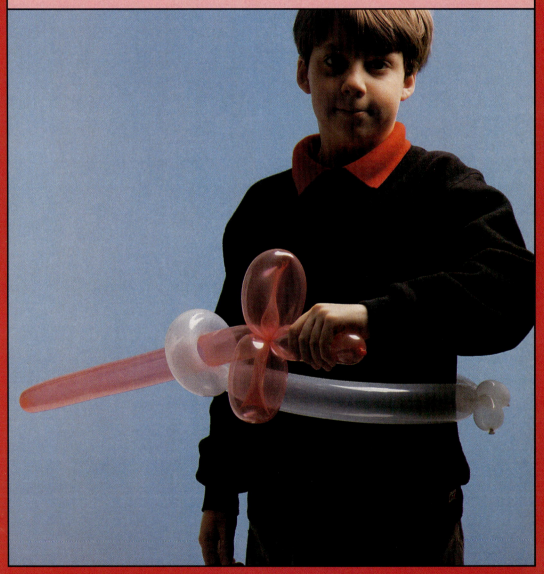

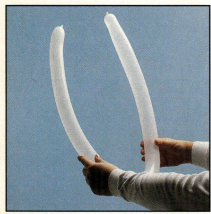

1. Begin by inflating a balloon, leaving a ½-inch tail.

2. Wrap the balloon around the waist of the child who'll wear the belt. Twist-connect the ends of the balloon.

3. Twist-connect the other side of the balloon belt to make a small loop. Twist this loop at least three times.

4. Inflate a second balloon, leaving a ½-inch tail.

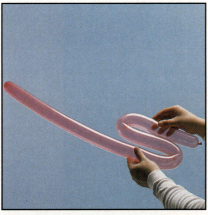

5. Fold the balloon to form an *S* at one end.

6. Twist the *S* in half to make two small loops.

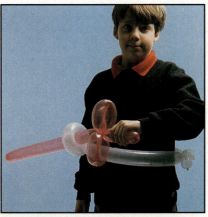

7. Slide the balloon sword through the loop of the belt to complete a pirate's belt and sword.

ELEPHANT

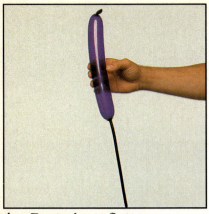

1. Begin by inflating a balloon, leaving an 8-inch tail.

2. Twist off three 1-inch bubbles.

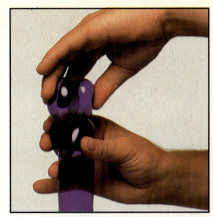

3. Twist-connect the second and third bubbles.

4. Twist off one 2-inch bubble and two 1-inch bubbles.

5. Twist-connect the two 1-inch bubbles.

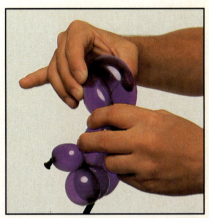

6. Twist off a 3-inch bubble, and fold-twist, as shown.

7. Twist off another 3-inch bubble and a 1-inch bubble. Fold-twist the 3-inch bubble.

8. The 1-inch bubble and the balloon's tail form your elephant's head and trunk.

1. To make a skull, you need a bee balloon, which can be purchased at most balloon and magic shops. Inflate a white bee balloon, and tie it off.

2. Twist off a large bubble.

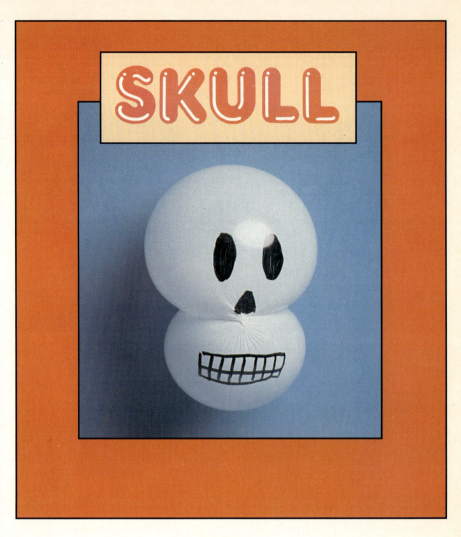

SKULL

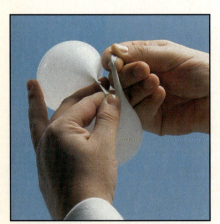

3. Fold the two bubbles, and tie the balloon's tail to its nozzle.

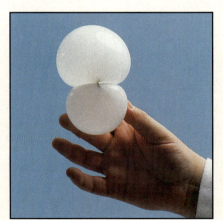

4. Turn the balloon over, and hold the large bubble on top.

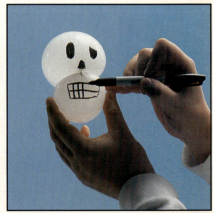

5. Use a laundry marker to draw a face and teeth.

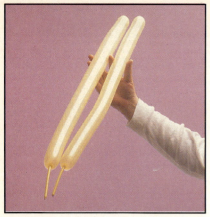

1. Begin by inflating two pencil balloons, leaving 5-inch tails.

2. Pinch a small bubble at the nozzle end of each balloon, and twist-connect.

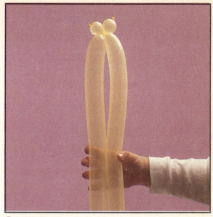

3. These bubbles will be used to lock the bee's antennae and wings.

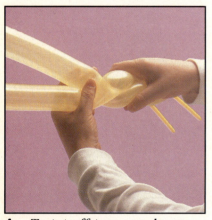

4. Twist off two very long bubbles on both balloons. Twist-connect the long bubbles.

5. Fold the long bubbles.

6. Twist-connect the long bubbles and small bubbles together.

7. Inflate and tie off a bee balloon. This kind of balloon is available at most balloon and magic shops.

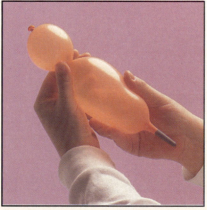

8. Twist off a bubble at the nozzle end as shown.

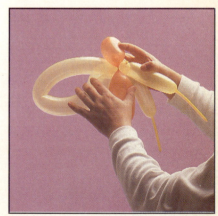

9. Twist-connect the wings to the bee's body below the bubble that's the bee's head.

10. Your bee is complete except for its antennae.

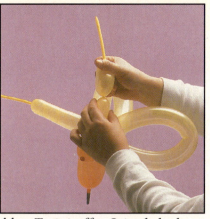

11. Twist off a 2-inch bubble, as shown.

12. Hold the 2-inch bubble with one hand and cradle the tail of the balloon with your other hand.

13. Squeeze the bubble hard to force air into the tip of the tail.

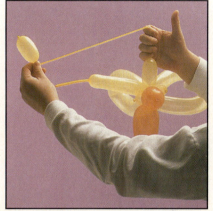

14. Hold the air in the bubble at the end of the tail. Stretch the balloon and release. Repeat steps 11, 12, 13, and 14 on the other antenna.

15. Use a laundry marker to draw eyes and stripes on your bee.

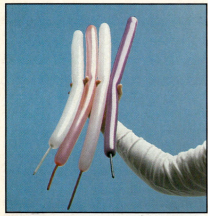

1. Begin by inflating four balloons, leaving 6-inch tails.

2. Twist-connect the four balloons at their nozzle ends.

3. Twist-connect the other ends, leaving a 6-inch bubble at the tail end of each balloon.

4. Twist off a 3-inch bubble, as shown.

5. Hold the balloon's tail in one hand and squeeze the 3-inch bubble with your other hand to move the bubble to the end of the tail.

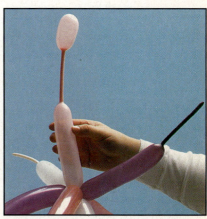

6. Hold the air in the bubble at the end of the tail. Stretch the balloon, then release it quickly.

7. Repeat steps 4, 5, and 6 on the three other balloons.

39

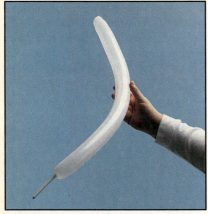

1. Begin by inflating a balloon, leaving a 4-inch tail.

2. Twist off one 1-inch bubble and two long bubbles.

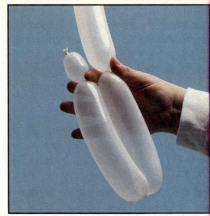

3. Twist-connect the two long bubbles.

4. The long bubbles are part of the swan's body; the 1-inch bubble is its tail.

5. Twist off another long bubble.

6. Pull the third long bubble between the two other long bubbles to complete the swan's body.

7. Fold the swan's neck to bend it.

8. Gently shape the swan's neck into a soft curve.

41

BIRD-BRAIN HAT

1. Begin by inflating four balloons, leaving 6-inch tails.

2. Twist-connect the four balloons at their nozzle ends.

3. Twist-connect the other ends, leaving a 6-inch bubble at the tail end of each balloon.

4. Twist off a 3-inch bubble, as shown.

5. Hold the tail of one of the balloons in one hand and squeeze the 3-inch bubble with your other hand to move the bubble to the end of the tail.

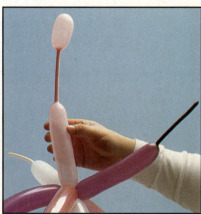

6. Hold the air in the bubble at end of the tail. Stretch the balloon, then release it quickly.

7. Repeat steps 4, 5, and 6 on the three other balloons.

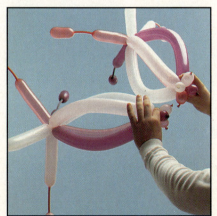

8. Make another party hat. Twist-connect the two hats at the nozzle ends.

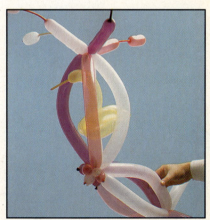

9. Slide a swan (or other animal) into the top hat.

BANANAS

1. Begin by inflating a balloon, leaving a 3½-inch tail.

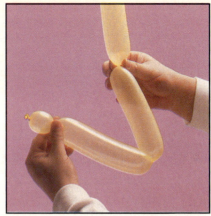

2. Twist off one small bubble and two long bubbles.

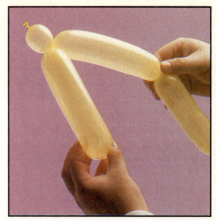

3. Twist-connect the two long bubbles.

4. Twist off another long bubble and roll it between the two other long bubbles.

5. Twist off one more long bubble.

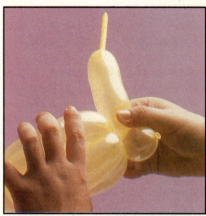

6. Twist-connect this long bubble with the small bubble.

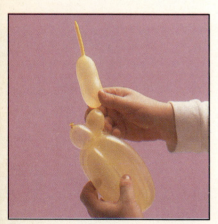

7. Twist off another small bubble.

8. Hold the two small bubbles, and carefully cut into the tail with scissors.

9. Tie a knot near the small bubbles, and cut off and discard the tail. You can also leave on the tail and use it to tie the bananas to a fruit basket.

45

PENGUIN

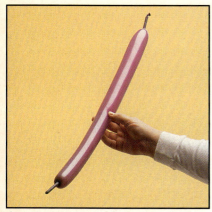

1. Begin by inflating a balloon, leaving a 2-inch tail. Then squeeze out air near the nozzle to make another 2-inch tail on this end of the balloon. Tie off the balloon.

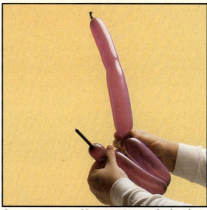

2. Twist off one 2-inch bubble and two long bubbles at the tail end of the balloon.

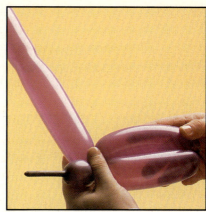

3. Twist-connect the two long bubbles.

4. Twist off another long bubble, and roll it between the two twist-connected long bubbles.

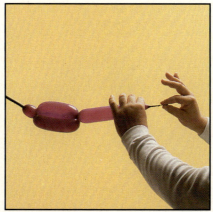

5. Pinch the knot, and pull it as close to the nozzle as you can.

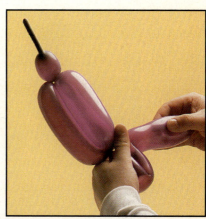

6. Twist off a 3-inch bubble, and fold-twist.

7. Twist off another 3-inch bubble, and fold-twist.

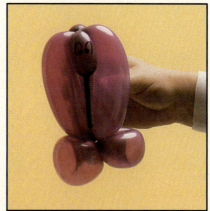

8. Pull the bubble with the tail on it between the two long bubbles to complete your penguin.

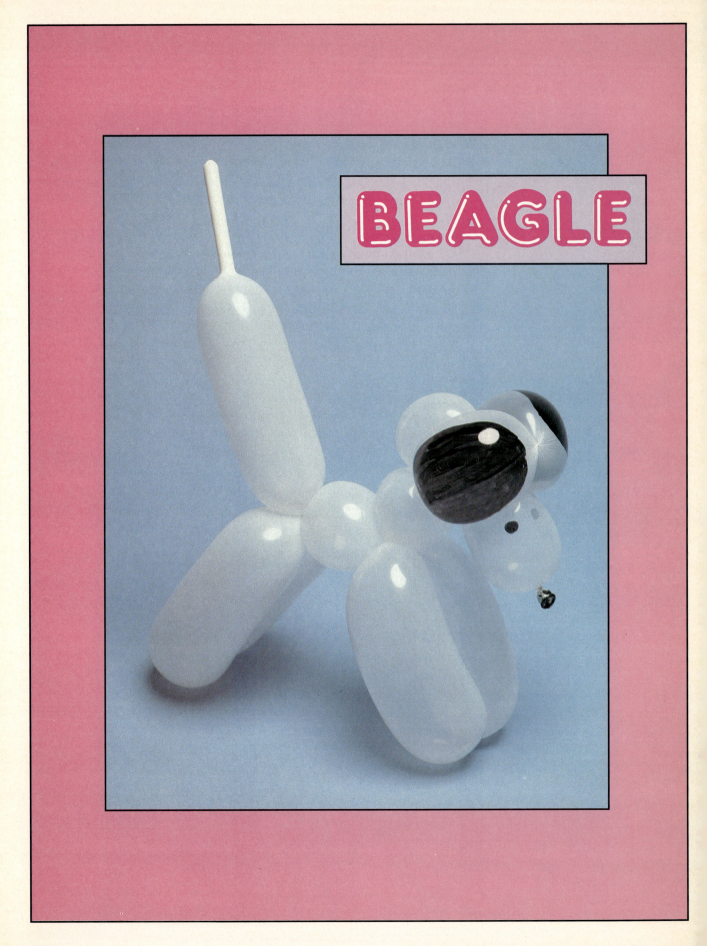

1. Begin by inflating a balloon, leaving a 5-inch tail.

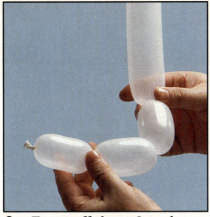

2. Twist off three 2-inch bubbles.

3. Twist-connect the second and third 2-inch bubbles.

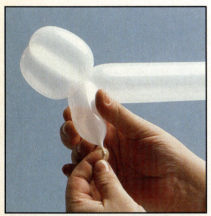

4. Pull the knot as close to the nozzle as you can to soften the first bubble.

5. Push half of the soft bubble between the twist-connected bubbles.

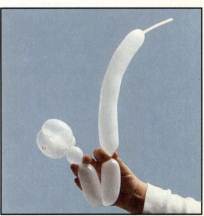

6. Twist off one 1-inch bubble and two 3-inch bubbles.

7. Twist-connect the two 3-inch bubbles.

8. Twist off one 1-inch bubble and two 3-inch bubbles.

9. Twist-connect the bubbles to complete your beagle.

FLOWER BRACELET

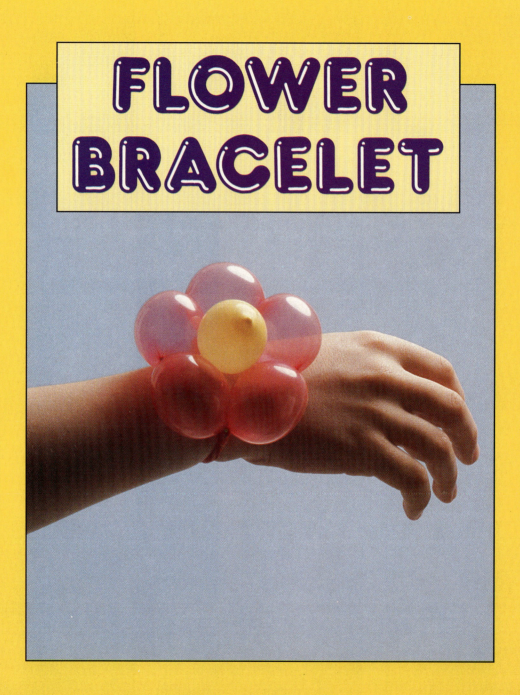

1. Begin by inflating a balloon, leaving a 9-inch tail.

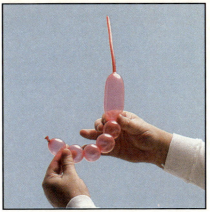
2. Twist off five 1-inch bubbles.

3. Hold the last bubble, and carefully cut the tail of the balloon.

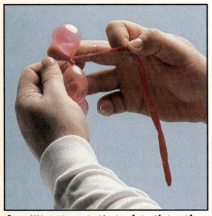
4. Tie the deflated tail to the balloon's nozzle.

5. Form a tight ring of bubbles.

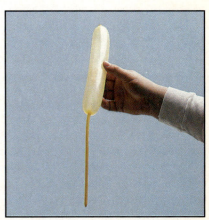
6. Inflate another balloon, leaving a 9-inch tail.

7. Twist off a 2-inch bubble, and hold it with one hand. Hold the tail with your other hand.

8. Squeeze the bubble. Guide the air up the tail to form a bubble at its tip.

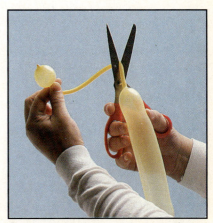
9. Pinch the tail below the bubble at the tip, hold the pinch, and cut the balloon.

(continued)

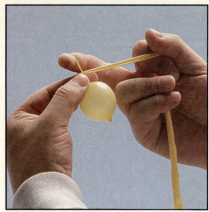

10. Tie a knot near the base of the bubble.

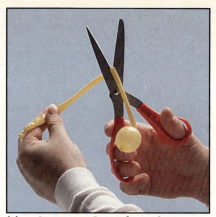

11. Leave a 3-inch tail on the bubble, and cut off the excess.

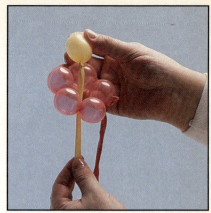

12. Pull the tail on the bubble through the ring of bubbles that you made with the first balloon.

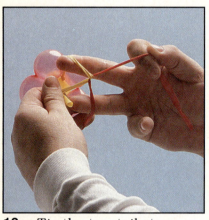

13. Tie the two tails together.

14. Trim the tails near the knot.

15. Pull the bubble out of the ring, and wrap the bracelet around someone's wrist.

16. Slide the bubble back into the ring of bubbles to complete the flower bracelet.

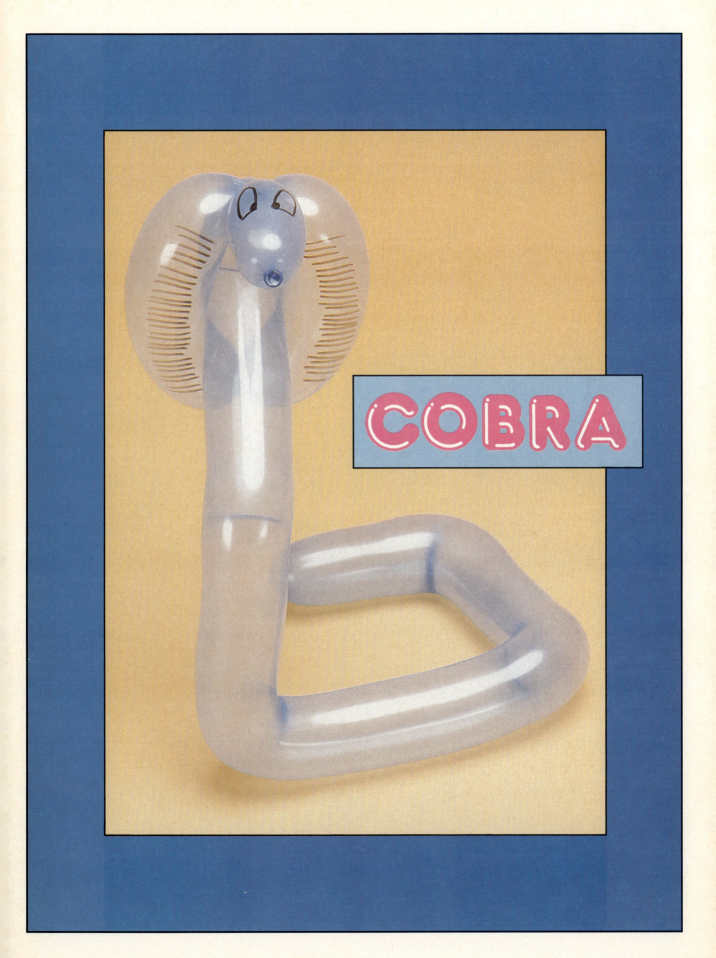

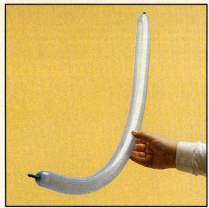
1. Begin by inflating a balloon, leaving a 1½-inch tail.

2. Twist off one 2-inch bubble and two long bubbles. Twist-connect the long bubbles.

3. Roll the top part of the balloon between the two long bubbles.

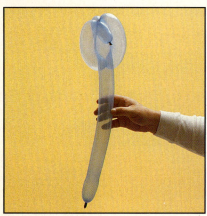
4. Your cobra's head should look like this.

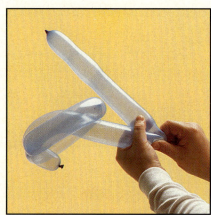
5. Pinch-twist the balloon 6 inches below the head.

6. Pinch-twist the balloon again a few inches from its tail end.

7. Use a laundry marker to draw eyes and decorate your cobra's hood.

LADYBUG

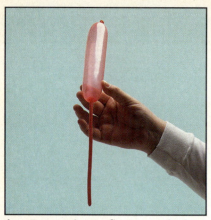

1. Begin by inflating a balloon, leaving a 10-inch tail.

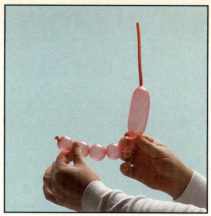

2. Twist off five 1-inch bubbles.

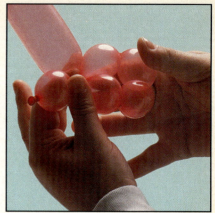

3. Twist-connect the first and last bubbles.

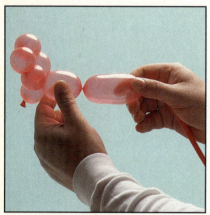

4. Twist off a 2-inch bubble.

5. Roll the 2-inch bubble through the twist-connected smaller bubbles.

6. Twist off a ½-inch bubble, and hold it. Cut a slit in the tail of the balloon.

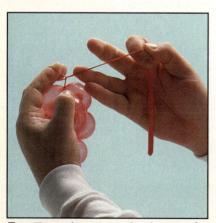

7. Tie a knot at the base of the ½-inch bubble.

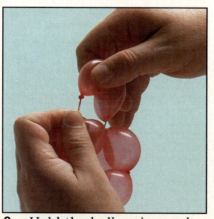

8. Hold the balloon's nozzle in one hand, and ear-twist the first bubble that you made.

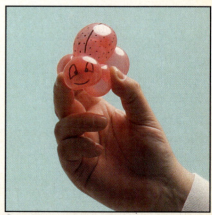

9. Use a laundry marker to give your ladybug a face and spots.

SCORPION

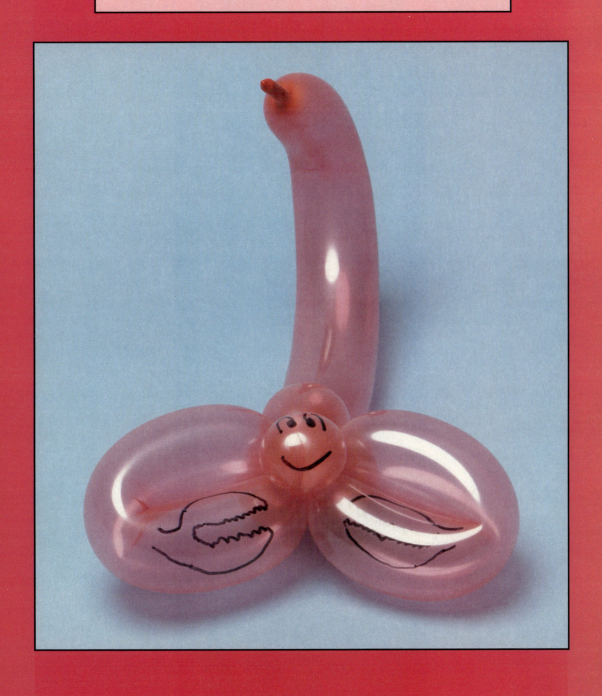

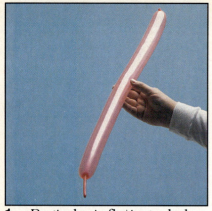

1. Begin by inflating a balloon, leaving a 3-inch tail.

2. Twist off a 2-inch bubble and a 5-inch bubble. Fold-twist the 5-inch bubble.

3. Twist off another 5-inch bubble.

4. Fold-twist the second 5-inch bubble.

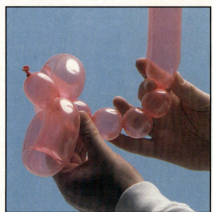

5. Twist off four 1-inch bubbles.

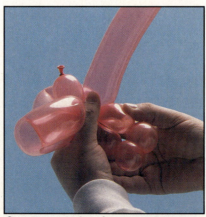

6. Bring the first and last 1-inch bubbles together.

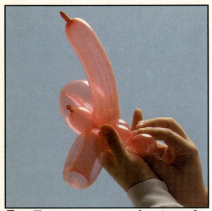

7. Twist-connect the 1-inch bubbles, as shown.

8. Twist off a 2-inch bubble, and roll it between the four 1-inch bubbles.

9. Fold the long bubble to curl the scorpion's tail.

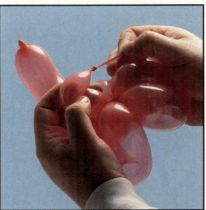

10. Take hold of the nozzle with one hand, and make an ear-twist in the first 2-inch bubble that you made. This forms the scorpion's head.

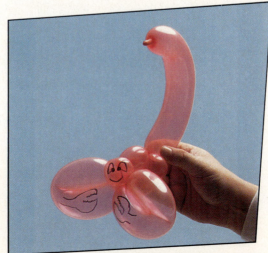

11. Use a laundry marker to draw a face and claws on your scorpion.

59

RABBIT IN HEART

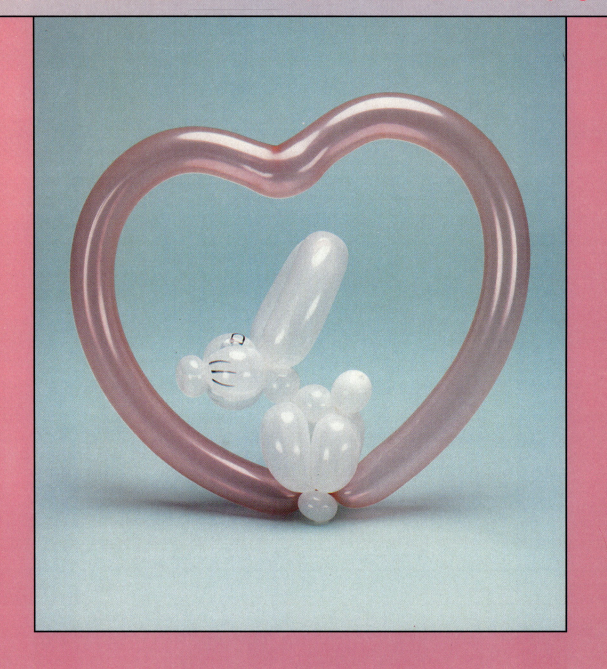

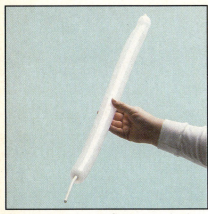

1. Begin by inflating a balloon, leaving a 4-inch tail.

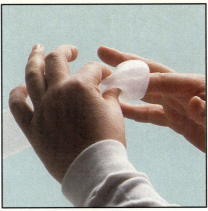

2. Push the knot into the balloon with your forefinger.

3. Grab the knot with your other hand, and remove your forefinger. Twist the bubble at least three times.

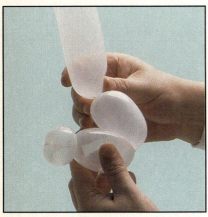

4. Twist off two 2-inch bubbles.

5. Twist-connect the two 2-inch bubbles.

6. Twist off another 2-inch bubble, and roll it between the two twist-connected bubbles.

7. Twist off two long bubbles.

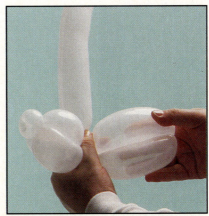

8. Twist-connect the two long bubbles.

(continued)

61

9. Your rabbit's head should look like this.

10. Twist off a 2-inch bubble, a ½-inch bubble, and another 2-inch bubble.

11. Twist-connect the two 2-inch bubbles.

12. Twist off a 1-inch bubble, a 2-inch bubble, a ½-inch bubble, and another 2-inch bubble. Twist-connect the two 2-inch bubbles to complete your rabbit.

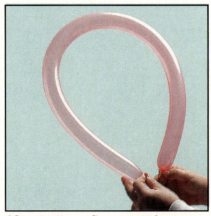

13. Fully inflate another balloon. Form a loop and tie both ends together.

14. Using both hands, pull the top of the loop toward the tied ends to form a heart.

15. Hold the folded balloon and slightly twist the point of the fold.

16. Put the rabbit in the heart by twisting the ½-inch bubbles together at the base of the heart.

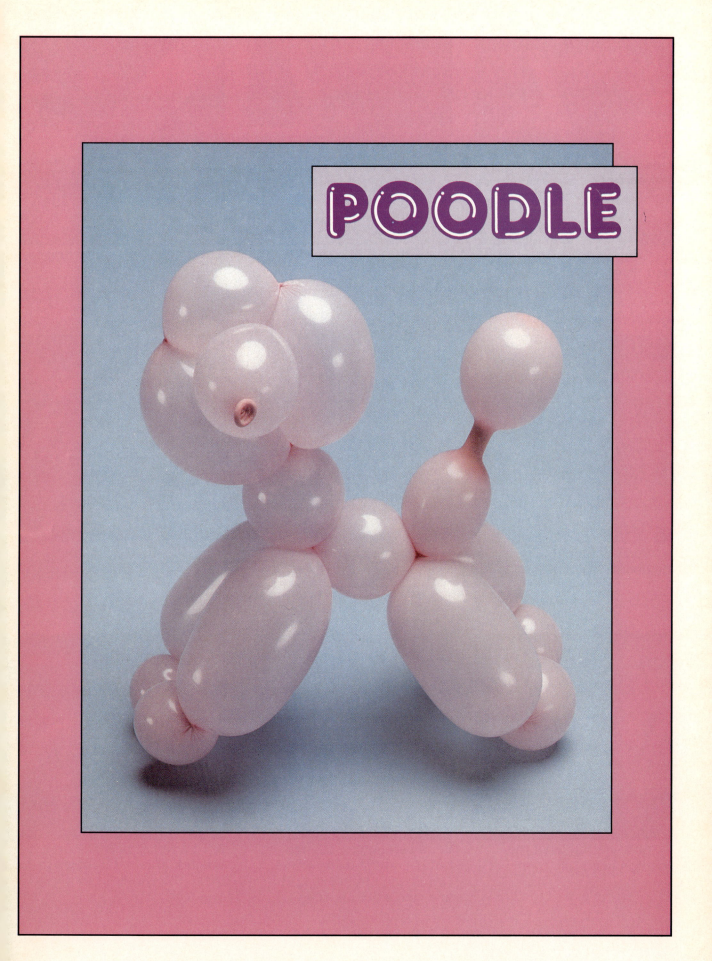

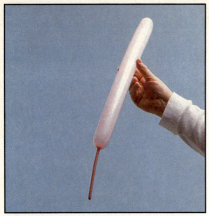

1. Begin by inflating a balloon, leaving a 6-inch tail.

2. Twist off a 2-inch bubble, a 1-inch bubble, a ½-inch bubble, and another 1-inch bubble.

3. Twist-connect the first and the last bubbles.

4. You've made the top of the poodle's head.

5. Pull the knot toward the balloon's nozzle to soften the 2-inch bubble.

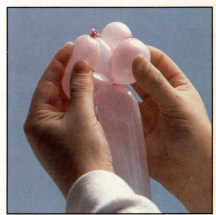

6. Roll half of the 2-inch bubble between the three other bubbles.

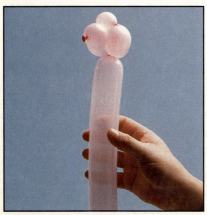

7. You've completed the poodle's head.

8. Twist off one ½-inch bubble, one 2-inch bubble, two ½-inch bubbles, and another 2-inch bubble.

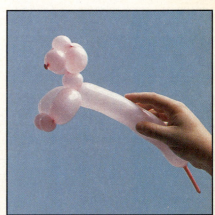

9. Twist-connect the first, second, and last bubbles to make the poodle's front legs and feet.

10. Twist off one 1-inch bubble, one 2-inch bubble, two ½-inch bubbles, and another 2-inch bubble.

11. Twist-connect the first, second, and last bubbles to make the poodle's body, back legs, and feet.

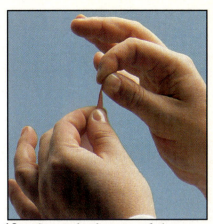

12. Stretch the tip of the tail.

13. Place your thumb and forefinger between the bubble that forms the tail and the tip.

14. Squeeze the bubble to force air into the tip of the balloon.

15. Hold on to the bubble, and give it a hard pull to keep air in the tip of the tail.

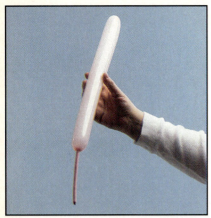

1. Begin by inflating a balloon, leaving a 6-inch tail.

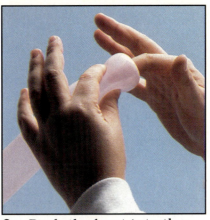

2. Push the knot into the balloon with your forefinger.

3. Hold the knot with your other hand, and gently remove your forefinger.

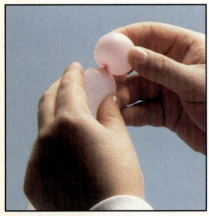

4. Twist the bubble at least three times.

5. Twist off six 1-inch bubbles.

6. Twist-connect the second and the last bubbles.

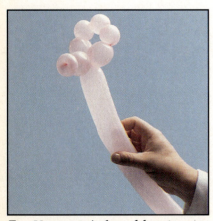

7. Your pig's head begins to take shape.

8. Push the apple-twisted bubble into the ring of bubbles.

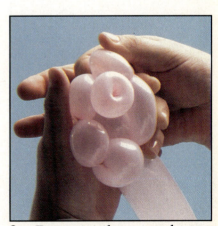

9. Ear-twist the second bubble on the top of the ring to make an ear.

(continued)

67

10. Ear-twist the fourth bubble on the top of the ring of bubbles to make the pig's other ear.

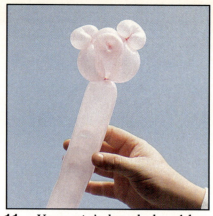
11. Your pig's head should look like this.

12. Twist off one 1-inch bubble and two 2-inch bubbles.

13. Twist-connect the 2-inch bubbles to form the pig's front legs.

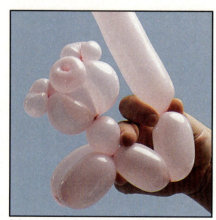
14. Twist off two 2-inch bubbles, and twist-connect.

15. Twist off another 2-inch bubble.

16. Roll the 2-inch bubble between the two twist-connected bubbles.

17. Twist off two more 2-inch bubbles.

18. Twist-connect the two 2-inch bubbles.

1. Begin by inflating a balloon, leaving a 4-inch tail.

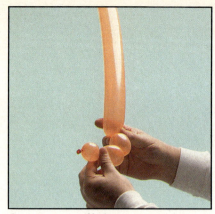

2. Twist off three 1-inch bubbles.

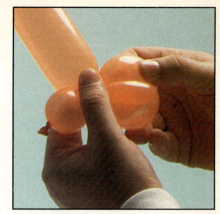

3. Twist-connect the second and third bubbles.

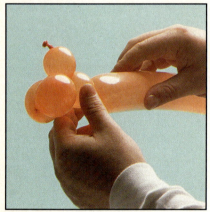

4. Twist off another 1-inch bubble.

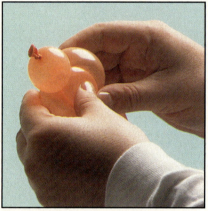

5. Roll the fourth 1-inch bubble between the two twist-connected bubbles.

6. Twist off six 1-inch bubbles.

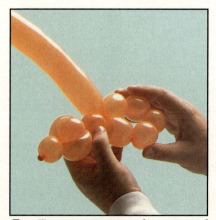

7. Twist-connect the second and sixth bubbles to make a ring of five bubbles.

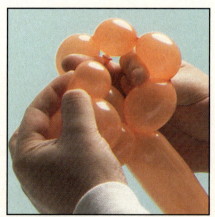

8. Open the ring with one hand. With your other hand, roll the first bubble that you made through the ring of bubbles.

70

9. Hold the bubbles in place with one hand.

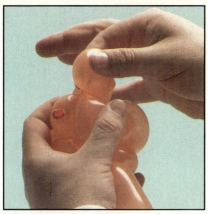

10. Ear-twist the two bubbles on either side of the tiger's head.

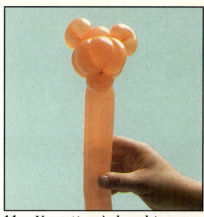

11. Your tiger's head is complete, so begin to make its body.

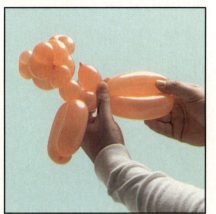

12. Twist off one ½-inch bubble and two 3-inch bubbles, and twist-connect the second and third bubbles. Then twist off another ½-inch bubble and two 3-inch bubbles, and twist-connect the second and third bubbles.

13. Use a laundry marker to draw the tiger's face and stripes.

71

CHRISTMAS WREATH

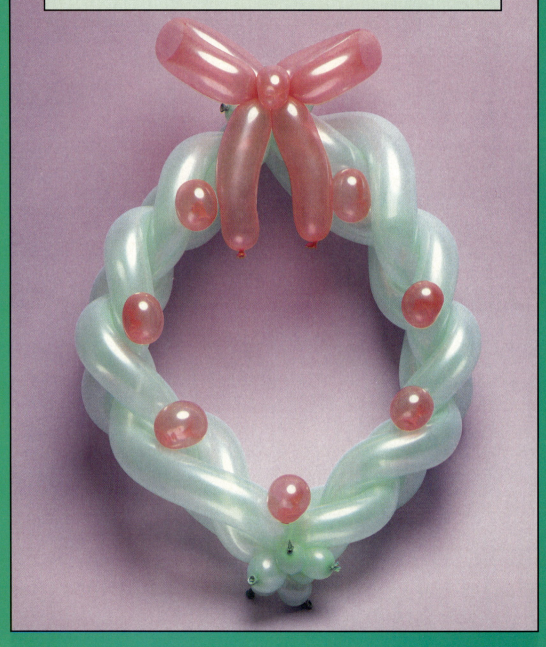

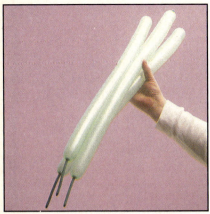
1. Begin by inflating three balloons, leaving 4-inch tails.

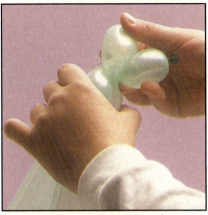
2. Twist-connect the three balloons at their nozzle ends.

3. Braid the three balloons.

4. Gently squeeze the balloons while you're braiding them to force air into the balloons' tails.

5. Pull the completed braid tight.

6. Twist-connect the balloons to hold the braid.

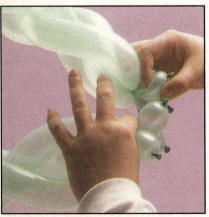
7. Using three more balloons, repeat steps 1, 2, 3, 4, 5, and 6. Twist-connect the six balloons together at the nozzle ends.

8. Twist-connect the tail ends.

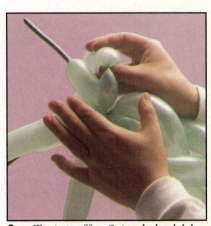
9. Twist off a 2-inch bubble on one of the balloons, as shown.

(continued)

73

10. Hold the 2-inch bubble. Cut the balloon's tail, and let it deflate down to the bubble that you're holding.

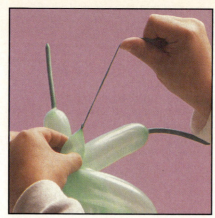

11. Tie the balloon near the bubble, and cut off the excess tail. Repeat steps 9, 10, and 11 on the five other balloons.

12. The wreath is complete and ready to decorate.

13. Inflate a balloon, leaving a 3-inch tail.

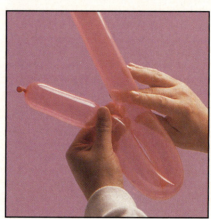

14. Twist off a 4-inch bubble and an 8-inch bubble.

15. Fold-twist the 8-inch bubble.

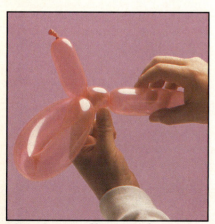

16. Twist off a 1-inch bubble.

17. Ear-twist the 1-inch bubble.

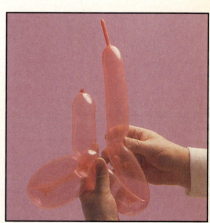

18. Twist off another 8-inch bubble.

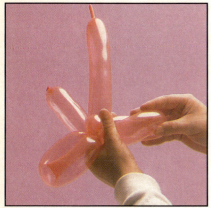

19. Fold-twist the 8-inch bubble.

20. Twist off a 4-inch bubble, and hold it. Cut the tail, and deflate the remaining bubble.

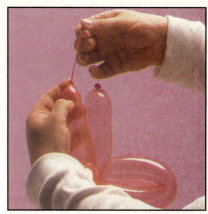

21. Tie off the 4-inch bubble with the deflated tail.

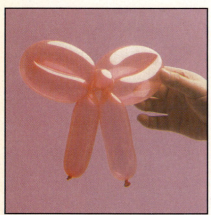

22. The bow is ready to be attached to the wreath.

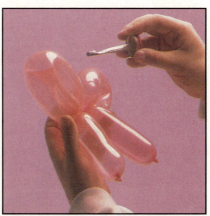

23. Apply rubber cement to the bow.

24. Attach the bow to the top of the wreath.

25. Inflate other balloons to make little bubbles.

26. Use rubber cement to attach the little bubbles to the wreath.

TEDDY BEAR

1. Begin by inflating a balloon, leaving a 4-inch tail.

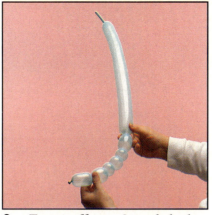

2. Twist off two 2-inch bubbles, three 1-inch bubbles, and another 2-inch bubble.

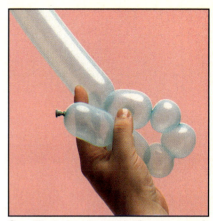

3. Twist-connect the second and the sixth bubbles.

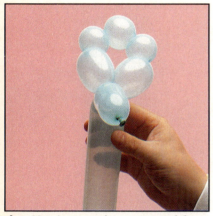

4. You've made a ring of five bubbles behind the first 2-inch bubble.

5. Pull the knot at the nozzle to soften the first bubble.

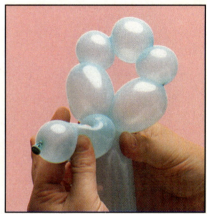

6. Grasp the first bubble between the thumb and forefinger of one hand.

7. Open the ring of bubbles with your other hand.

8. Push the first bubble through the ring, and hold it in place.

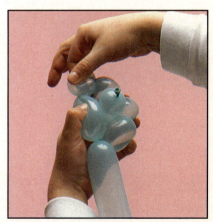

9. Ear-twist the first 1-inch bubble, as shown.

(continued)

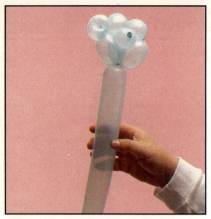

10. Your teddy bear now has one ear.

11. Ear-twist the 1-inch bubble on the other side of the bear's head.

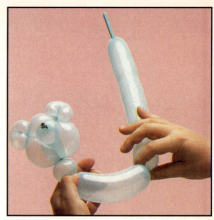

12. Twist off a 1-inch bubble and a 4-inch bubble.

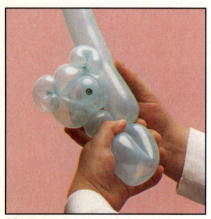

13. Fold-twist the 4-inch bubble.

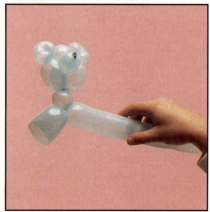

14. The 4-inch bubble becomes one of the teddy bear's arms.

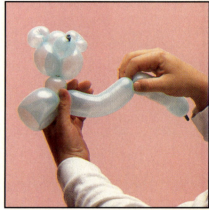

15. Twist off another 4-inch bubble.

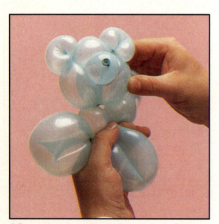

16. Fold-twist the 4-inch bubble.

17. Gently position the bear's arms, as shown.

18. Repeat steps 12, 13, 14, 15, and 16 to complete your teddy bear.

HUGS 'N' KISSES

1. Begin by inflating three round balloons. Tie them off, and then tie them together.

2. Inflate another round balloon, and tie it off. Apple-twist the balloon by pushing the knot into the balloon with your forefinger until you can feel the knot on the other side. Grab the knot with your other hand and twist; secure with clear tape. Rubber cement the balloons together, as shown.

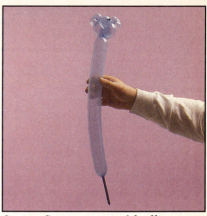

3. Inflate a pencil balloon, leaving a 4-inch tail. Make a teddy bear's head, following steps 2 through 11 on pages 77–78.

4. Make the teddy bear's forelegs by twisting off one 1-inch bubble, one 2-inch bubble, two ½-inch bubbles, and another 2-inch bubble. Twist-connect the 2-inch bubbles.

5. Twist off one 1-inch bubble, one 2-inch bubble, two ½-inch bubbles, and another 2-inch bubble. Twist-connect the 2-inch bubbles.

6. Twist off a 1-inch bubble, and hold it. Carefully cut off the leftover bubble, and tie off the balloon near the 1-inch bubble.

7. Make another teddy bear by repeating steps 3, 4, 5, and 6.

8. Open the forelegs of one of the teddy bears, and roll them over the head of the other bear.

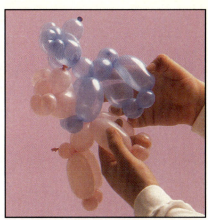
9. Slide the back legs of the second teddy bear through the forelegs of the first bear.

10. Tie the nozzles of the teddy bears together. Make a heart, following steps 1, 2, and 3 on page 14.

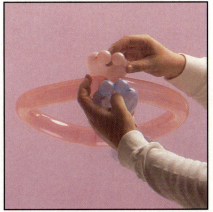
11. Attach the two teddy bears to the heart by twisting their feet together.

12. Twist the bears so that they stand up in the heart.

13. To complete the centerpiece, use rubber cement to attach the heart to the balloon base, and add a flower.

FLOWER

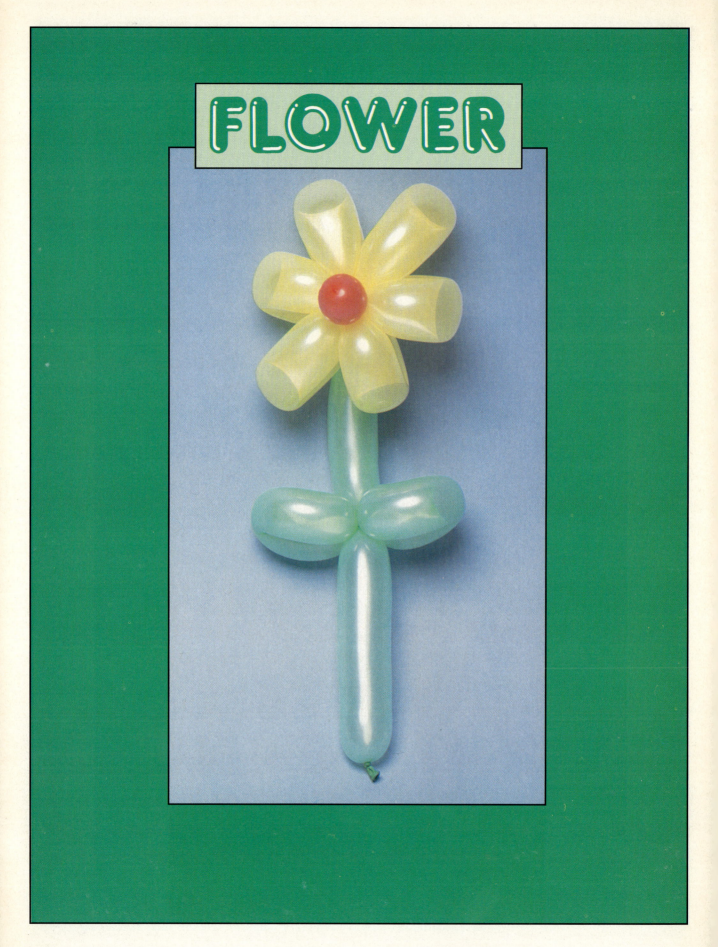

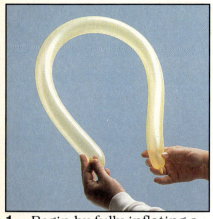
1. Begin by fully inflating a balloon, but don't tie it off.

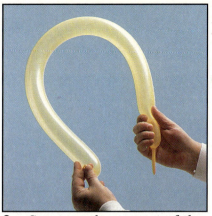
2. Squeeze the air out of the balloon's tail end, leaving a 3-inch tail.

3. Tie the nozzle to the tip of the tail.

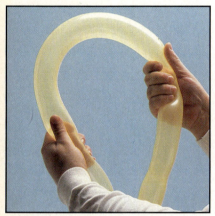
4. Squeeze the loop to soften it.

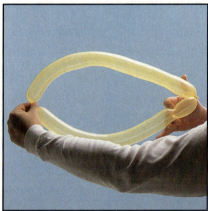
5. Divide the loop in half.

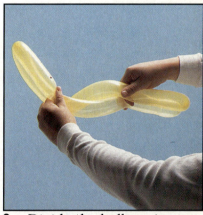
6. Divide the balloon in thirds, as shown.

7. Twist to make three smaller divided loops.

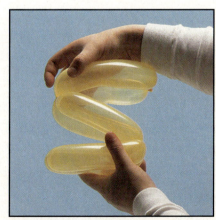
8. Fold the balloon in the shape of a *Z*.

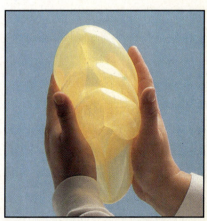
9. Push the top and bottom of the *Z* together.

(continued)

83

10. Twist the top three folds at least two times.

11. The twist becomes the center of a flower with six petals.

12. Inflate another balloon, and make a poodle-tail twist. Pinch the balloon to hold the bubble, and cut the tail.

13. Tie the balloon at the bubble, leaving a long deflated tail.

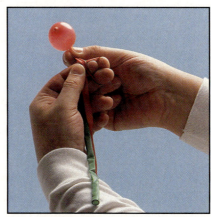

14. Tie the bubble to a balloon that hasn't been inflated.

15. Cut off the bubble's excess tail. Be careful not to cut into the uninflated balloon.

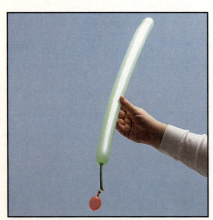

16. Inflate the uninflated balloon, leaving a 3-inch tail.

17. Pull the tied-off bubble into the center of the flower.

18. Make two fold-twists in the balloon that's the flower's stem to form leaves.

1. Begin by inflating a balloon, leaving a 5-inch tail.

2. Twist off a 2-inch bubble and a 1-inch bubble at the nozzle end of the balloon.

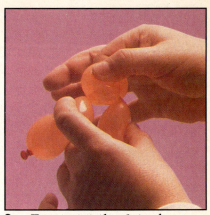
3. Ear-twist the 1-inch bubble.

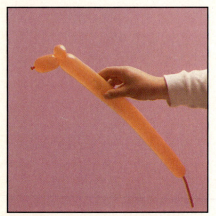
4. The ear-twisted bubble forms one side of the clown's hat brim.

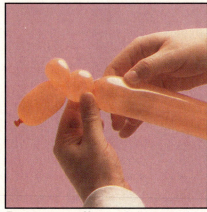
5. Twist off another 1-inch bubble, and ear-twist it to complete the clown's hat.

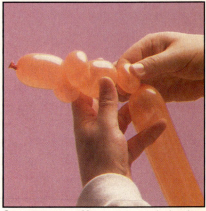
6. Twist off two 1-inch bubbles.

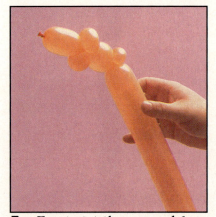
7. Ear-twist the second 1-inch bubble. Twist off another 1-inch bubble, and ear-twist it.

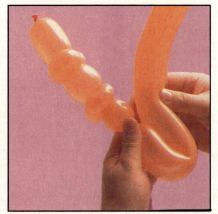
8. Twist off a 1-inch bubble and a 4-inch bubble. Fold-twist the 4-inch bubble.

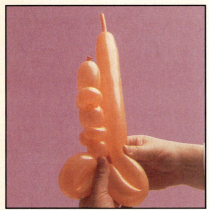

9. Twist off another 4-inch bubble, and fold-twist it.

10. The fold-twisted 4-inch bubbles form the clown's arms.

11. Twist off a 1-inch bubble and a 4-inch bubble. Fold-twist the 4-inch bubble.

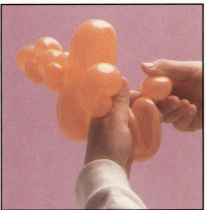

12. Twist off another 4-inch bubble, and fold-twist it. The extra little bubble is a locking bubble.

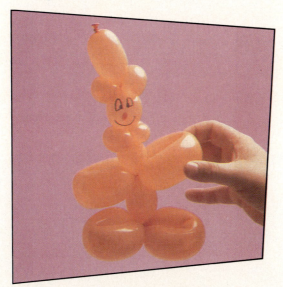

13. Use two colors of laundry marker to draw the clown's face.

AIRPLANE

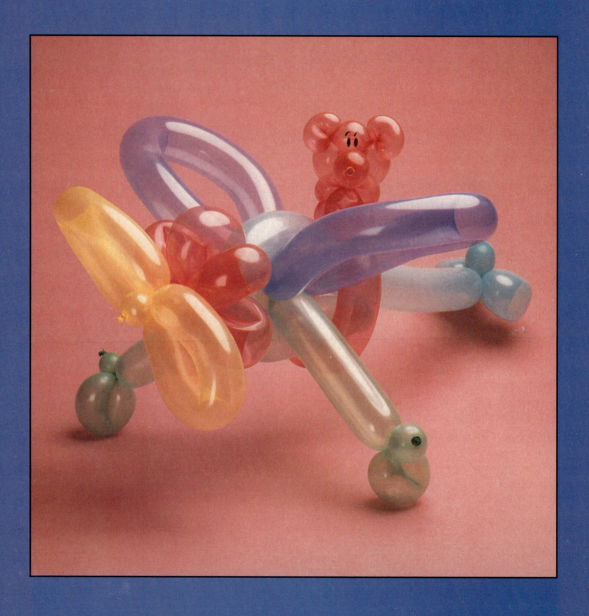

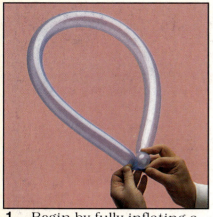

1. Begin by fully inflating a balloon. Tie the ends together to form a loop.

2. Divide this loop in half to make two smaller loops. Twist to hold the loops in place.

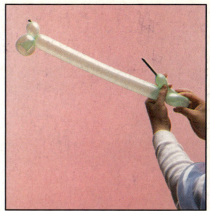

3. Inflate another balloon, leaving a 3-inch tail. Make two fold-twists on each end of the balloon, as shown. Tie off the excess tail, and cut it off.

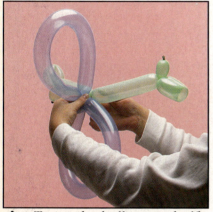

4. Twist the balloon in half, and connect it between the two loops on the first balloon, as shown.

5. The wings and landing gear of your airplane should look like this.

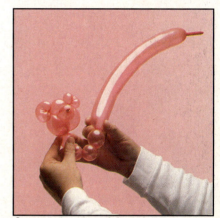

6. Make a teddy bear's head, following steps 1 through 11 on pages 77–78, then twist off four 1-inch bubbles.

7. Twist-connect the first and last 1-inch bubbles.

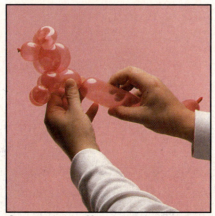

8. Twist off a 2-inch bubble.

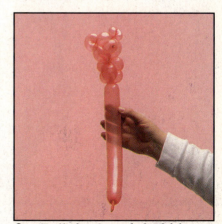

9. Roll the 2-inch bubble through the four twist-connected bubbles.

(continued)

89

10. Twist off two long bubbles, and twist-connect.

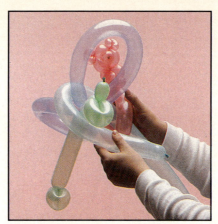

11. Fully inflate another balloon and pull it through the bear's legs. Wrap the balloon over the wings and around the landing gear.

12. Slide the balloon back through the teddy bear's legs.

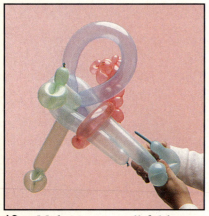

13. Make two small fold-twists at the tail end of the balloon, as shown.

14. The airplane's motor is made in the same way as the petals of the flower. Follow steps 1 through 11 on pages 83–84.

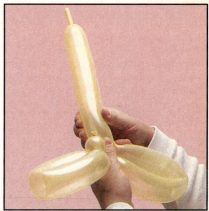

15. Inflate another balloon, leaving a 3-inch tail. Twist off one 1-inch bubble and two 8-inch bubbles. Fold-twist the 8-inch bubbles.

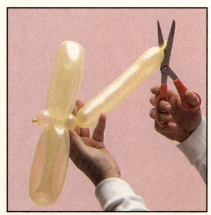

16. Twist off a 1-inch bubble, and hold it. Cut the long bubble, and tie off the balloon near the 1-inch bubble. Don't remove the excess balloon.

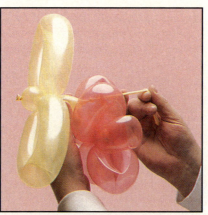

17. Pull the balloon's deflated tail into the center of the flower to form the airplane's propeller and motor.

18. Pull the deflated tail on the propeller through the loop at the front of the plane's fuselage. Tie the motor and propeller securely in place.

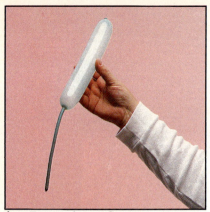

1. Begin by inflating a balloon, leaving a 7-inch tail.

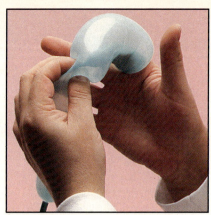

2. Make a hook-twist. Push the knot into the balloon with your forefinger. Your entire finger should be inside the balloon.

3. Grab the knot of the balloon with the fingers of your other hand, and carefully roll the balloon off your forefinger.

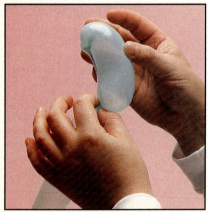

4. Twist this odd-shaped bubble at least 3 times.

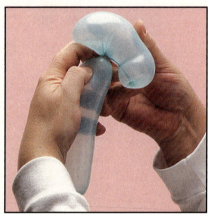

5. Push the knot a quarter of the way into the bubble.

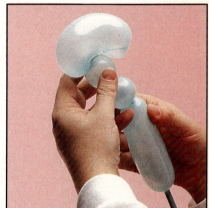

6. To make the frog's legs, twist off two 1-inch bubbles.

7. Hold the two 1-inch bubbles together.

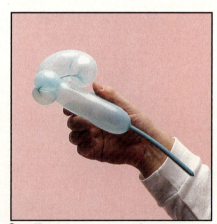

8. Twist-connect the two bubbles.

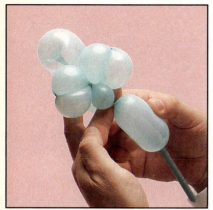
9. Twist off two more 1-inch bubbles, and twist-connect them. Twist off one ½-inch bubble.

10. Hold the small bubble, and carefully cut the balloon's tail.

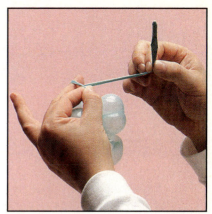
11. Tie a knot close to the small bubble, and trim off the excess balloon.

12. Go back to the hook-twisted bubble, and twist off a small bubble.

13. Twist the bubble you've just made in half to make the frog's eyes.

14. Use a laundry marker to draw a face and markings on your frog.

93

ALIEN

1. Begin by inflating a balloon, leaving a 5-inch tail.

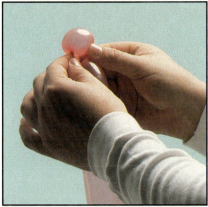

2. Twist off a 1-inch bubble. Hold the nozzle, and give the bubble an ear-twist.

3. Draw eyes on the bubble with a laundry marker.

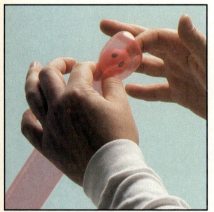

4. Push the 1-inch bubble into the balloon, and make an apple-twist by holding the knot while you remove your forefinger.

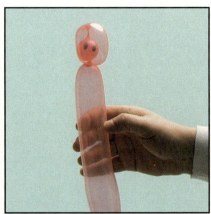

5. Twist the bubble three times to hold the alien's head inside his helmet.

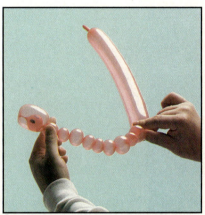

6. Twist off nine 1-inch bubbles.

7. Twist-connect the first and last 1-inch bubbles to make a ring of nine bubbles.

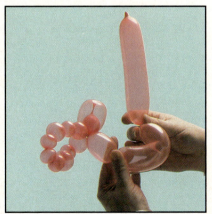

8. Twist off one 2-inch bubble and two 5-inch bubbles.

(continued)

95

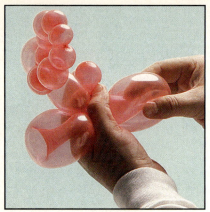

9. Fold-twist the 5-inch bubbles.

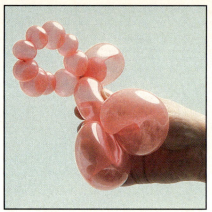

10. The 5-inch bubbles form the alien's legs.

11. Go back to the ring of nine bubbles. Ear-twist the second, fourth, sixth, and eighth bubbles.

12. Twist the fourth and sixth bubbles in half.

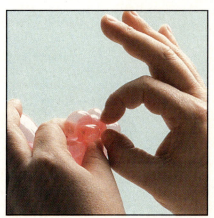

13. Complete a pop-twist by breaking the fifth bubble to make the alien's arms.

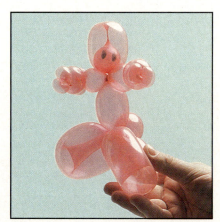

14. Gently twist the alien until he takes the position you want.

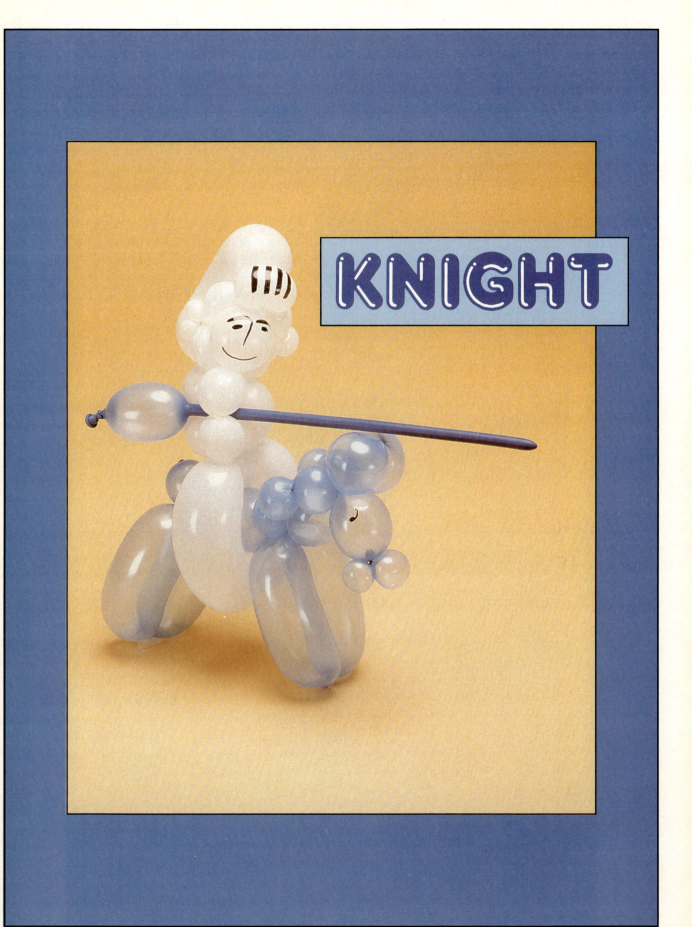

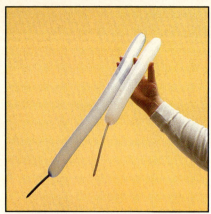

1. Begin by inflating two balloons. Leave an 8-inch tail on one and a 4-inch tail on the other.

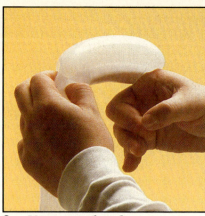

2. Use your forefinger to push the knot into the balloon with the 8-inch tail.

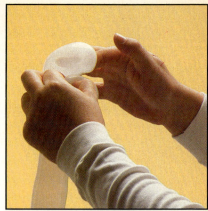

3. Hold the knot with your other hand while you withdraw your finger.

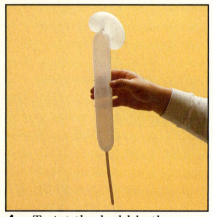

4. Twist the bubble three times, and push the knot into the bubble to complete a hook-twist.

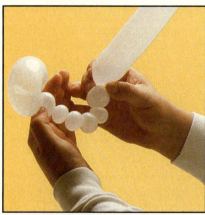

5. Twist off six ½-inch bubbles.

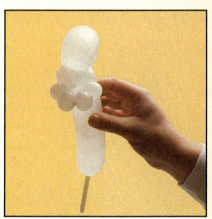

6. Twist-connect the first and last bubbles to form a ring of six bubbles.

7. Twist off a 1-inch bubble.

8. Ear-twist the 1-inch bubble.

9. Twist off another 1-inch bubble.

10. Roll the 1-inch bubble into the ring of six ½-inch bubbles.

11. Twist the hook-twisted bubble to the back of the ring.

12. Ear-twist the second and fourth bubbles on the ring of six ½-inch bubbles.

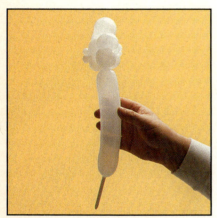
13. You've completed the knight's head with his helmet and plume.

14. Twist off four 1-inch bubbles.

15. Twist connect the first and last bubbles.

16. Twist off a 1-inch bubble, and roll it through the ring of four 1-inch bubbles.

17. Twist off two 2-inch bubbles, and twist-connect them.

18. Use a laundry marker to draw the knight's face and visor.

(continued)

19. Use the balloon with the 4-inch tail to make the knight's horse. Make an apple-twist at the nozzle end, and divide the bubble in half.

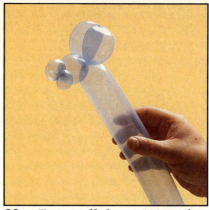

20. Twist off three 1½-inch bubbles, and twist-connect the second and third bubbles.

21. Twist off six 1-inch bubbles, and twist-connect the first and last bubbles to form a ring of six bubbles.

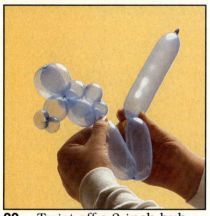

22. Twist off a 2-inch bubble, and roll it through the ring of bubbles to complete the horse's head and neck. Twist off two 2-inch bubbles, and twist-connect them to the horse's neck.

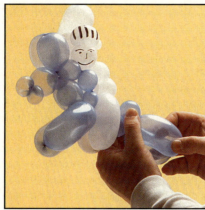

23. Slide the knight onto the horse. Twist-connect two 2-inch bubbles and one 1-inch bubble to form the horse's back legs and tail.

24. Slide a drinking straw inside an uninflated balloon.

25. Inflate the balloon to make a 2-inch bubble, and tie it off.

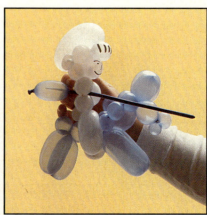

26. Slide the lance through the knight's arm.

SANTA CLAUS

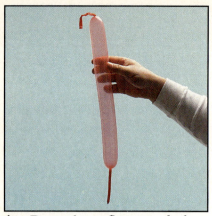

1. Begin by inflating a balloon, leaving a 4-inch tail. Squeeze air out of the balloon through the nozzle, leaving 3 inches of deflated balloon. Knot the balloon near the nozzle.

2. Make an apple-twist by pushing the knot into the balloon with your forefinger. Hold the knot with your other hand while you remove your finger. Twist the bubble at least three times.

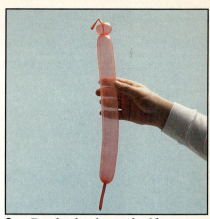

3. Push the knot halfway back into the bubble. The nozzle end of the balloon should extend beyond the apple-twist to form the tassel on Santa's hat.

4. Twist off one 1-inch bubble, one ½-inch bubble, and two 1-inch bubbles.

5. Ear-twist the ½-inch bubble and the last two 1-inch bubbles.

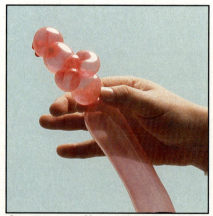

6. Twist off another 1-inch bubble.

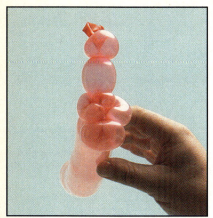

7. Ear-twist this 1-inch bubble to complete Santa's head.

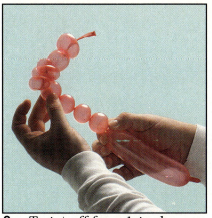

8. Twist off four 1-inch bubbles, and twist-connect the first and last bubbles to make a ring of four bubbles.

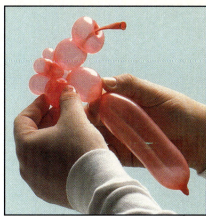

9. Twist off one 2-inch bubble, and roll it into the ring of four 1-inch bubbles.

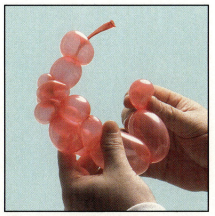

10. Twist off two 2½-inch bubbles, and twist-connect them.

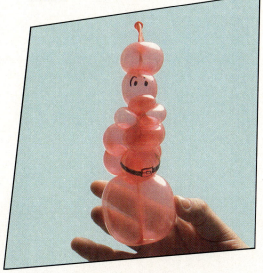

11. Draw a face and belt on the balloon with a laundry marker to complete your Santa Claus.

UNICORN

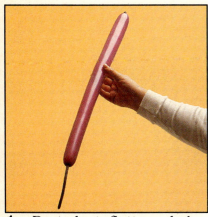

1. Begin by inflating a balloon, leaving a 5-inch tail.

2. Push the knot into the balloon with your forefinger.

3. Hold the knot with your other hand, and gently remove your forefinger. Twist the bubble at least three times to complete an apple-twist.

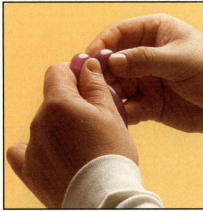

4. Divide the apple-twisted bubble in half.

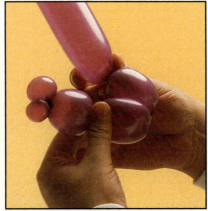

5. Twist off three 1½-inch bubbles, and twist-connect the second and third bubbles.

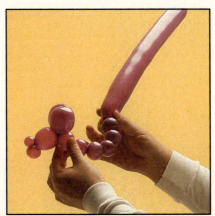

6. Twist off six 1-inch bubbles, and twist-connect the first and last bubbles to make a ring of six bubbles.

(continued)

105

7. Twist off a 2-inch bubble.

8. Roll the 2-inch bubble through the ring of six bubbles.

9. Add a body by twisting off one 1-inch bubble and two 2-inch bubbles. Twist-connect the 2-inch bubbles. Then twist off another 1-inch bubble and two 2-inch bubbles, and twist-connect the 2-inch bubbles.

10. Cut a drinking straw about 3 inches long, and drop it into an uninflated balloon. Don't inflate the balloon. Tie it off at the straw, and cut off the excess balloon with scissors.

11. Slide the unicorn's horn between its ears.

REINDEER

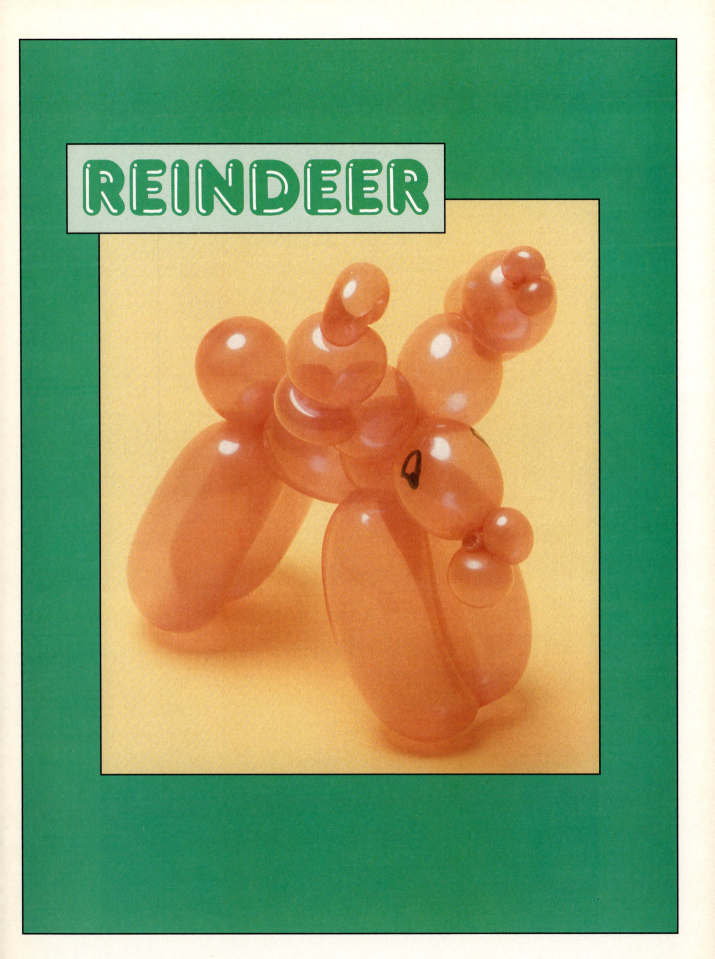

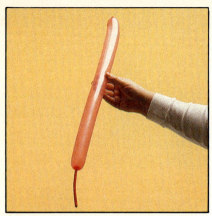

1. Begin by inflating a balloon, leaving a 5-inch tail.

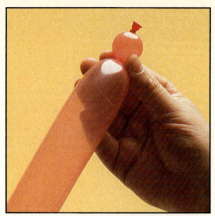

2. Twist off a ½-inch bubble at the nozzle end of the balloon.

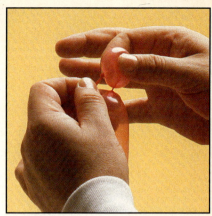

3. Hold the nozzle, and ear-twist the ½-inch bubble.

4. Twist the ear-twisted bubble in half.

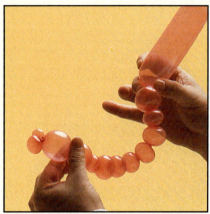

5. Twist off one 2-inch bubble and nine 1-inch bubbles.

6. Twist-connect the first and last 1-inch bubbles.

7. The nine 1-inch bubbles form a ring that will become the reindeer's antlers.

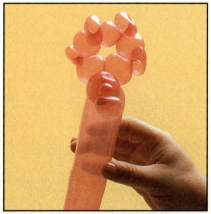

8. Ear-twist the second, fourth, sixth, and eighth bubbles in the ring of nine bubbles.

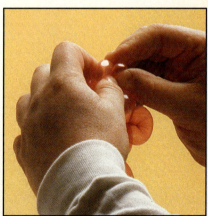

9. Twist the fourth and sixth bubbles in half.

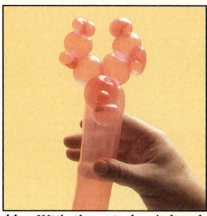

10. Pop the fifth bubble to complete a pop-twist, and separate the reindeer's two antlers.

11. With the reindeer's head complete, go on to make its body.

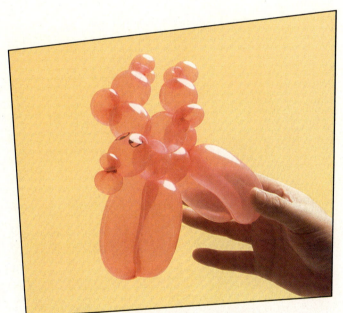

12. Twist off one ½-inch bubble and two 3-inch bubbles, and twist-connect the second and third bubbles. Then twist off another ½-inch bubble and two 3-inch bubbles, and twist-connect the second and third bubbles.

109

BASEBALL PLAYER

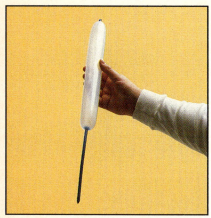

1. Begin by inflating a balloon, leaving an 8-inch tail.

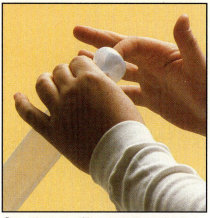

2. Twist off a small bubble at the nozzle end of the balloon, and make an apple-twist.

3. Twist off a 1-inch bubble.

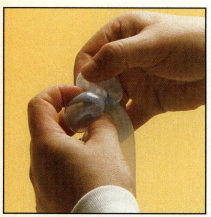

4. Ear-twist the 1-inch bubble. This completes the baseball player's cap.

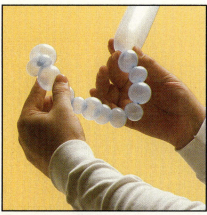

5. Twist off one 1-inch bubble, then make nine ½-inch bubbles. Twist-connect the first and last ½-inch bubbles to form a ring of nine bubbles.

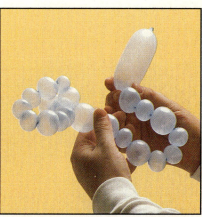

6. Twist off one 1-inch bubble and nine ½-inch bubbles. Twist-connect the first and last ½-inch bubbles to form another ring of nine bubbles.

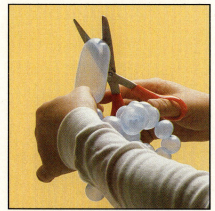

7. Twist off one ½-inch bubble, and hold it. Very carefully cut off the remaining inflated balloon.

8. Knot the balloon at the ½-inch bubble that you're holding.

(continued)

111

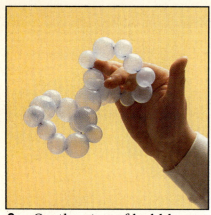

9. On the ring of bubbles near the cap, ear-twist the second, fourth, sixth, and eighth bubbles.

10. Repeat step 9 on the other ring of bubbles.

11. On each ring, twist the fourth and sixth bubbles in half, and pop the fifth bubble.

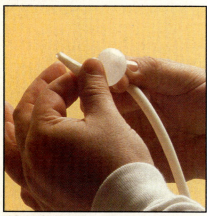

12. To make a baseball, inflate a balloon to make a tiny bubble.

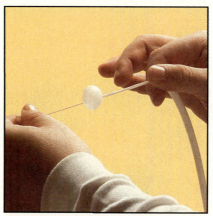

13. Tie off the balloon on both sides of the bubble. Cut off both the tail and the nozzle ends. Using a laundry marker, draw lines on the bubble to represent the baseball's stitching.

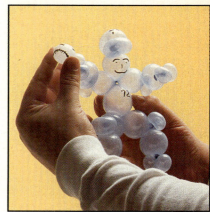

14. Draw a face and number on the baseball player. Use rubber cement to attach the ball to his hand.

PARATROOPER

FAT CLOWN

1. Begin by inflating a balloon, leaving a 2-inch tail.

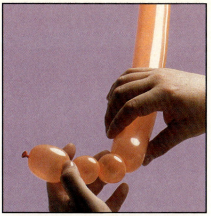
2. Twist off one 2-inch bubble and two 1-inch bubbles.

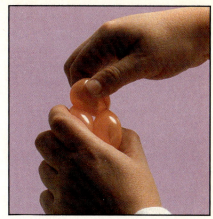
3. Ear-twist the 1-inch bubbles.

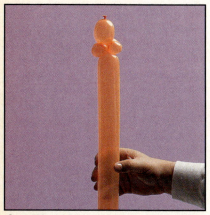
4. The clown's hat should look like this.

5. Twist off two 1-inch bubbles, and hold them.

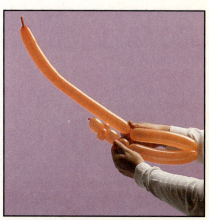
6. Twist off two long bubbles.

7. Twist-connect the two long bubbles.

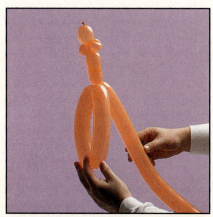
8. Let go of the two 1-inch bubbles to make one soft bubble.

9. Twist off another long bubble, and roll it between the two other long bubbles.

(continued)

115

10. Twist off a 1-inch bubble.

11. Ear-twist the 1-inch bubble.

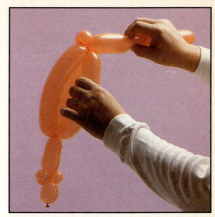

12. Pop the unused portion of the balloon as shown.

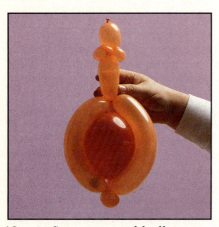

13. Inflate a round balloon, and place it in the center of the long bubbles to form the clown's belly.

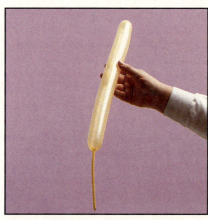

14. Inflate a balloon, leaving a 6-inch tail.

15. Twist 13 1-inch bubbles.

16. Counting from the nozzle, ear-twist bubbles 2, 4, 6, 9, 11, and 13.

17. Twist off another 1-inch bubble, and ear-twist it.

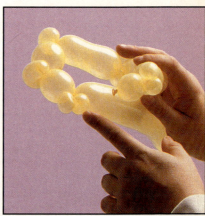

18. Twist bubbles 2 and 13 in half.

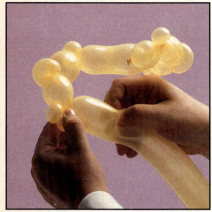

19. Pop the first bubble and the end of the balloon.

20. Your clown's arms should look like this.

21. Twist-connect the clown's arms to his body, as shown.

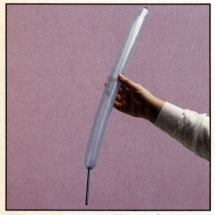

22. Inflate a balloon, leaving a 4-inch tail.

23. Twist off 12 1-inch bubbles, and ear-twist bubbles 2, 4, 6, 8, 10, and 12.

24. Twist the second and last bubbles in half, and pop the long bubble at the nozzle end of the balloon.

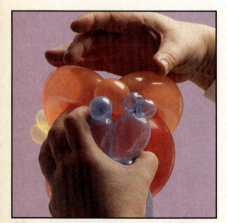

25. Attach the ends of the balloon to the bubble at the bottom of the clown's body.

26. Pop the bubble between the ear-twisted bubbles to separate the clown's legs.

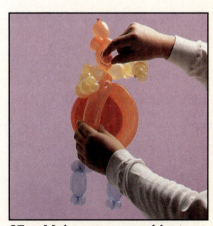

27. Make a nose and buttons with little bubbles. Use rubber cement to attach the bubbles to the clown. Draw the clown's eyes and smile with a laundry marker.

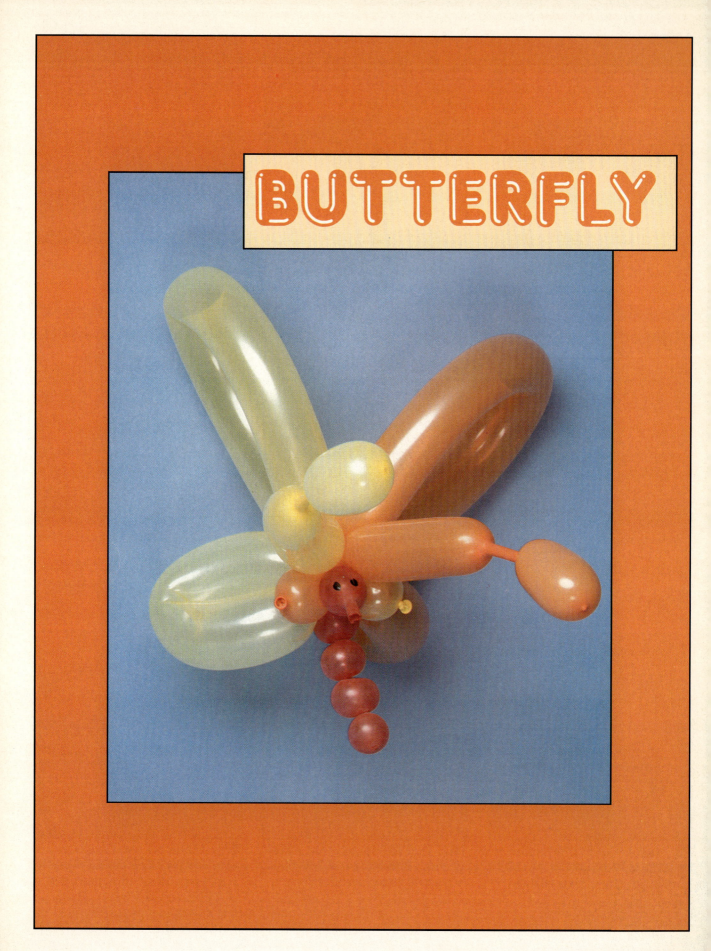

1. Begin by inflating a balloon, leaving a 9-inch tail.

2. Twist off a ½-inch bubble, and push it into the balloon.

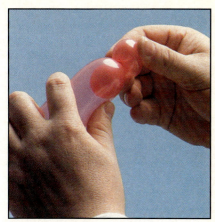

3. Twist off a second ½-inch bubble, and push it into the balloon.

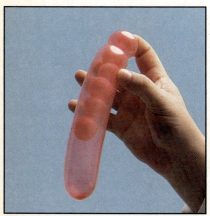

4. Continue to make bubbles, and push them inside the balloon until you run out of balloon. Apple-twist the last bubble.

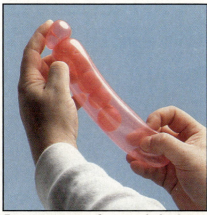

5. A string of ½-inch bubbles is inside the balloon. The apple-twisted bubble is outside. Pinch the balloon to pop it.

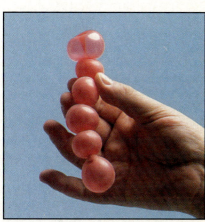

6. The string of bubbles forms the head and body of the butterfly.

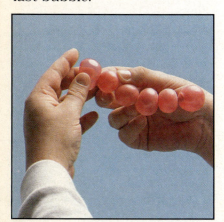

7. Untwist the apple-twist.

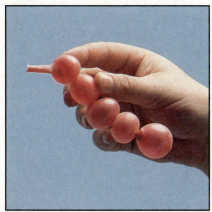

8. Your butterfly now has a proboscis.

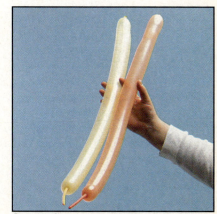

9. Inflate two balloons, leaving 5-inch tails.

(continued)

119

10. Twist-connect the two balloons at their nozzle ends, forming two 2-inch bubbles.

11. Fold the two balloons.

12. Twist-connect the loops to the bubbles.

13. Twist-connect the other ends of the balloons.

14. Twist-connect the large loops to the smaller loops and the bubbles.

15. Twist off a 2-inch bubble at the top of one of the long bubbles.

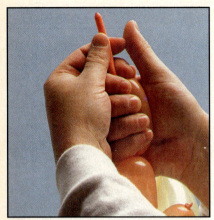
16. Hold the tail gently with one hand, and squeeze the 2-inch bubble.

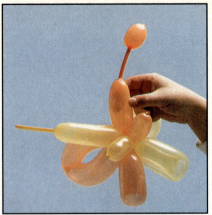
17. The bubble is now at the tip of the balloon's tail. Repeat the poodle-tail twist to make the butterfly's other antenna.

18. Twist-connect the butterfly's body to its antennae and wings.

19. Use a laundry marker to draw eyes on your butterfly.

20. Your butterfly is complete.

1. To make a big swan, you'll need 340 airship balloons. You can buy them at most balloon and magic stores. Begin by inflating two 340 airship balloons, leaving 1-inch tails.

2. Tie the ends of the balloons together to form a large loop.

3. Twist the loop in half.

4. Pull one of the small loops into the other.

5. Lock this arrangement by pulling one long bubble around the other.

6. The swan's body should look like this.

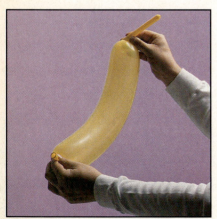

7. Inflate a 340 airship balloon, leaving a 4-inch tail.

8. Tie the ends together.

9. Twist the folded balloon in half.

(continued)

123

10. Connect this balloon to the swan's body by twisting it around the two long bubbles.

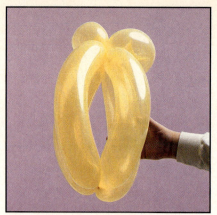

11. The swan's body and tail should look like this.

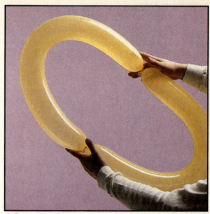

12. Inflate two 340 airship balloons, leaving 1-inch tails. Tie the ends of the balloons together to form a large loop, and twist the loop in half.

13. Push the double loop into the body of the swan.

14. The swan's body with wings looks like this.

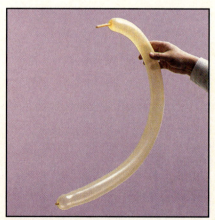

15. Inflate a pencil balloon, leaving a 3-inch tail.

16. Curl the tail end of the balloon.

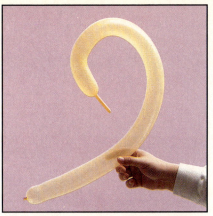

17. Release the tight curl to make a gentle arch.

18. Curl the nozzle end in the opposite direction, and release the curl.

19. Twist off a 1-inch bubble near the nozzle.

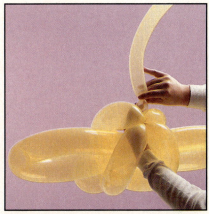

20. Twist-connect the 1-inch bubble on the pencil balloon to the front of the swan's body by wrapping the small bubble around one of the long bubbles.

21. Gently squeeze the balloons to shape the swan the way you want it.

125

FRUIT BASKET

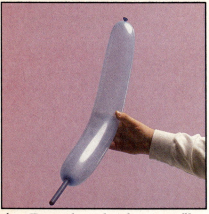

1. To make a basket, you'll need 340 airship balloons, which you can purchase at most balloon and magic shops. Inflate a 340 airship balloon, leaving a 3-inch tail.

2. Twist off two 2-inch bubbles.

3. Ear-twist the second bubble.

4. Twist off a long bubble and a 2-inch bubble.

5. Twist off another long bubble and a 2-inch bubble. Twist-connect the second 2-inch bubble and the last 2-inch bubble.

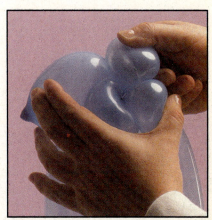

6. Ear-twist the last 2-inch bubble.

7. Pop the remaining bubble, as shown.

8. Ear-twist the 2-inch bubble at the other end of the basket.

9. Repeat steps 1 through 8 to make the other side of the basket.

(continued)

10. Twist-connect both ends of the two balloons.

11. Bury the nozzles by wrapping them around the bubbles.

12. Inflate a pencil balloon, leaving a 2-inch tail. Then squeeze out air near the nozzle to make a 2-inch tail. Tie off the balloon.

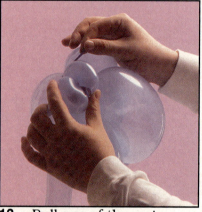
13. Pull one of the uninflated ends of the pencil balloon around the bubbles on one side of the basket, and wrap it securely in place.

14. Repeat step 13 on the other end of the basket to form a handle.

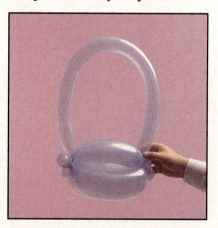

15. Your completed basket is ready to be decorated. Add flower bracelets to the handle, and attach a flower or a bow to the top. Fill the basket with balloon fruit, flowers, or animals.